Workshop on Software Engineering, Testing, and Quality Assurance for Natural Language Processing 2009

(SETQA-NLP 2009)

Held at NAACL HLT 2009

Boulder, Colorado, USA
5 June 2009

ISBN: 978-1-61738-569-8

Printed from e-media with permission by:

Curran Associates, Inc.
57 Morehouse Lane
Red Hook, NY 12571
www.proceedings.com

Some format issues inherent in the e-media version may also appear in this print version.

Printed by Curran Associates, Inc. (2010)

Association for Computational Linguistics
209 N. Eighth Street
Stroudsburg, Pennsylvania 18360

Phone: 1-570-476-8006
Fax: 1-570-476-0860

acl@aclweb.org

Introduction

Software engineering is a first-class research topic in computer science, but generally has not been treated as such within the natural language processing community. However, the need for well-engineered NLP components is increasing as NLP begins to show up outside our research community: bioinformatics, the search industry, education applications, etc. In addition, NLP research itself, e.g., when it involves large data sets, often requires a high level of software quality. Simply applying standard software engineering practices to NLP often fails due to the unique characteristics of natural language as an input type.

The goals of this workshop include raising awareness of the need for good software engineering practices in NLP, stimulating research on same, and providing a forum for sharing current work in this area. We are grateful to the authors for sharing their work, our invited speaker, and to the program committee for their efforts.

Kevin Bretonnel Cohen and Marc Light

Organizers:

Kevin Bretonnel Cohen, Center for Computational Pharmacology, University of Colorado School of Medicine and The MITRE Corporation

Marc Light, Thomson Reuters

Program Committee:

William A. Baumgartner Jr., University of Colorado School of Medicine
Shannon Bradshaw, Drew University
Bob Carpenter, Alias-i
Hamish Cunningham, University of Sheffield
Dan Flickinger, Stanford University
Michael Gamon, Microsoft
Tracy Holloway King, Microsoft/PowerSet
James Lyle, Microsoft
Stephan Oepen, Stanford University
Jeff Reynar, DBT Labs
Kevin Markey, Silver Creek Systems
Charles Schafer, Google
Jun'ichi Tsujii, University of Tokyo and UK National Centre for Text Mining
Martin Volk, University of Stockholm
Scott Waterman, Microsoft/PowerSet
Ken Williams, Thomson Reuters

Invited Speaker:

Ted Pedersen, University of Minnesota Duluth

Table of Contents

Conference Program

Friday, June 5, 2009

9:00–9:30 *Building Test Suites for UIMA Components*
Philip Ogren and Steven Bethard

9:30–10:00 *Context-Dependent Regression Testing for Natural Language Processing*
Elaine Farrow and Myroslava O. Dzikovska

10:00–10:30 *Using Paraphrases of Deep Semantic Representions to Support Regression Testing in Spoken Dialogue Systems*
Beth Ann Hockey and Manny Rayner

10:30–11:00 Morning Break

11:00–11:30 *Integrated NLP Evaluation System for Pluggable Evaluation Metrics with Extensive Interoperable Toolkit*
Yoshinobu Kano, Luke McCrohon, Sophia Ananiadou and Jun'ichi Tsujii

11:30–12:00 *Tightly Packed Tries: How to Fit Large Models into Memory, and Make them Load Fast, Too*
Ulrich Germann, Eric Joanis and Samuel Larkin

12:00–12:30 Poster Session

Scaling up a NLU system from text to dialogue understanding
Rodolfo Delmonte, Antonella Bristot, Gloria Voltolina and Vincenzo Pallotta

Towards Agile and Test-Driven Development in NLP Applications
Jana Sukkarieh and Jyoti Kamal

Grammar Engineering for CCG using Ant and XSLT
Scott Martin, Rajakrishnan Rajkumar and Michael White

12:30–2:00 Lunch Break

2:00–3:00 Invited Talk by Ted Pedersen: The road from good software engineering to good science ... is a two way street

3:00–3:30 *Web Service Integration for Next Generation Localisation*
David Lewis, Stephen Curran, Kevin Feeney, Zohar Etzioni, John Keeney, Andy Way and Reinhard Schäler

Friday, June 5, 2009 (continued)

3:30–4:00 Afternoon Break

4:00–4:30 *Distributed Parse Mining*
Scott Waterman

4:30–5:00 *Modular resource development and diagnostic evaluation framework for fast NLP system improvement*
Gaël de Chalendar and Damien Nouvel

5:00–5:30 *Integrating High Precision Rules with Statistical Sequence Classifiers for Accuracy and Speed*
Wenhui Liao, Marc Light and Sriharsha Veeramachaneni

Building Test Suites for UIMA Components

Philip V. Ogren
Center for Computational Pharmacology
University of Colorado Denver
Denver, CO 80217, USA
philip@ogren.info

Steven J. Bethard
Department of Computer Science
Stanford University
Stanford, CA 94305, USA
bethard@stanford.edu

Abstract

We summarize our experiences building a comprehensive suite of tests for a statistical natural language processing toolkit, ClearTK. We describe some of the challenges we encountered, introduce a software project that emerged from these efforts, summarize our resulting test suite, and discuss some of the lessons learned.

1 Introduction

We are actively developing a software toolkit for statistical natural processing called ClearTK (Ogren et al., 2008) [1], which is built on top of the Unstructured Information Management Architecture (UIMA) (Ferrucci and Lally, 2004). From the beginning of the project, we have built and maintained a comprehensive test suite for the ClearTK components. This test suite has proved to be invaluable as our APIs and implementations have evolved and matured. As is common with early-stage software projects, our code has undergone number of significant refactoring changes and such changes invariably break code that was previously working. We have found that our test suite has made it much easier to identify problems introduced by refactoring in addition to preemptively discovering bugs that are present in new code. We have also observed anecdotally that code that is more thoroughly tested as measured by code coverage has proven to be more reliable and easier to maintain.

While this test suite has been an indispensable resource for our project, we have found creating tests for our UIMA components to be challenging for a number of reasons. In a typical UIMA processing pipeline, components created by developers are instantiated by a UIMA container called the Collection Processing Manager (CPM) which decides at runtime how to instantiate components and what order they should run via configuration information provided in descriptor files. This pattern is typical of programming frameworks: the developer creates components that satisfy some API specification and then these components are managed by the framework. This means that the developer rarely directly instantiates the components that are developed and simple programs consisting of e.g. a main method are uncommon and can be awkward to create. This is indeed consistent with our experiences with UIMA. While this is generally a favorable approach for system development and deployment, it presents challenges to the developer that wants to isolate specific components (or classes that support them) for unit or functional testing purposes.

2 Testing UIMA Components

UIMA coordinates data generated and consumed by different components using a data structure called the Common Analysis Structure (CAS). The

[1] http://cleartk.googlecode.com

Proceedings of the NAACL HLT Workshop on Software Engineering, Testing, and Quality Assurance for Natural Language Processing, pages 1–4,
Boulder, Colorado, June 2009.

CAS represents the current state of analysis that has been performed on the data being analyzed. As a simple example, a UIMA component that performs tokenization on text would add token annotations to the CAS. A subsequent component such as a part-of-speech tagger would read the token annotations from the CAS and update them with part-of-speech labels. We have found that many of our tests involve making assertions on the contents of the CAS after a component or series of components has been executed for a given set of configuration parameters and input data. As such, the test must obtain an instance of a CAS after it has been passed through the components relevant to the tests.

For very simple scenarios a single descriptor file can be written which specifies all the configuration parameters necessary to instantiate a UIMA component, create a CAS instance, and process the CAS with the component. Creating and processing a CAS from such a descriptor file takes 5-10 lines of Java code, plus 30-50 lines of XML for the descriptor file. This is not a large overhead if there is a single test per component, however, testing a variety of parameter settings for each component results in a proliferation of descriptor files. These descriptor files can be difficult to maintain in an evolving codebase because they are tightly coupled with the Java components they describe, yet most code refactoring tools fail to update the XML descriptor when they modify the Java code. As a result, the test suite can become unreliable unless substantial manual effort is applied to maintain the descriptor files.

Thus, for ease of refactoring and to minimize the number of additional files required, it made sense to put most of the testing code in Java instead of XML. But the UIMA framework does not make it easy to instantiate components or create CAS objects without an XML descriptor, so even for relatively simple scenarios we found ourselves writing dozens of lines of setup code before we could even start to make assertions about the expected contents of a CAS. Fortunately, much of this code was similar across test cases, so as the ClearTK test suite grew, we consolidated the common testing code. The end result was a number of utility classes which allow UIMA components to be instantiated and run over CAS objects in just 5-10 lines of Java code. We decided that these utilities could also ease testing for projects other than ClearTK, so we created the UUTUC project, which provides our UIMA unit test utility code.

3 UUTUC

UUTUC[2] provides a number of convenience classes for instantiating, running, and testing UIMA components without the overhead of the typical UIMA processing pipeline and without the need to provide XML descriptor files.

Note that UUTUC cannot isolate components entirely from UIMA – it is still necessary, for example, to create AnalysisEngine objects, JCas objects, Annotation objects, etc. Even if it were possible to isolate components entirely from UIMA, this would generally be undesirable as it would result in testing components in a different environment from that of their expected runtime. Instead, UUTUC makes it easier to create UIMA objects entirely in Java code, without having to create the various XML descriptor files that are usually required by UIMA.

Figure 1 provides a complete code listing for a test of a UIMA component we wrote that provides a simple wrapper around the widely used Snowball stemmer[3]. A complete understanding of this code would require detailed UIMA background that is outside the scope this paper. In short, however, the code creates a UIMA component from the `SnowballStemmer` class, fills a CAS with text and tokens, processes this CAS with the stemmer, and checks that the tokens were stemmed as expected. Here are some of the highlights of how UUTUC made this easier:

Line 3 uses `TypeSystemDescriptionFactory` to create a `TypeSystemDescription` from the user-defined annotation classes `Token` and `Sentence`. Without this factory, a 10 line XML descriptor would have been required.

Line 5 uses `AnalysisEngineFactory` to create an `AnalysisEngine` component from the user-defined annotator class `SnowballStemmer` and the type system description, setting the stemmer name parameter to `"English"`. Without this factory, a 40-50 line XML descriptor would have been required (and near duplicate descrip-

[2] http://uutuc.googlecode.com – provided under BSD license
[3] http://snowball.tartarus.org

```
 1 @Test
 2 public void testSimple() throws UIMAException {
 3     TypeSystemDescription typeSystemDescription = TypeSystemDescriptionFactory
 4         .createTypeSystemDescription(Token.class, Sentence.class);
 5     AnalysisEngine engine = AnalysisEngineFactory.createAnalysisEngine(
 6         SnowballStemmer.class, typeSystemDescription,
 7         SnowballStemmer.PARAM_STEMMER_NAME, "English");
 8     JCas jCas = engine.newJCas();
 9     String text =   "The brown foxes jumped quickly over the lazy dog.";
10     String tokens = "The brown foxes jumped quickly over the lazy dog .";
11     TokenFactory.createTokens(jCas, text, Token.class, Sentence.class, tokens);
12     engine.process(jCas);
13     List<String> actual = new ArrayList<String>();
14     for (Token token: AnnotationRetrieval.getAnnotations(jCas, Token.class)) {
15         actual.add(token.getStem());
16     }
17     String expected = "the brown fox jump quick over the lazi dog .";
18     Assert.assertEquals(Arrays.asList(expected.split(" ")), actual);
19 }
```
Figure 1: A complete test case using UUTUC.

tor files would have been required for each additional parameter setting tested).

Line 11 uses `TokenFactory` to set the text of the CAS object and to populate it with `Token` and `Sentence` annotations. Creating these annotations and adding them to the CAS manually would have taken about 20 lines of Java code, including many character offsets that would have to be manually adjusted any time the test case was changed.

While a Python programmer might not be impressed with the brevity of this code, anyone who has written Java test code for UIMA components will appreciate the simplicity of this test over an approach that does not make use of the UUTUC utility classes.

4 Results

The test suite we created for ClearTK was built using UUTUC and JUnit version 4[4] and consists of 92 class definitions (i.e. files that end in *.java*) containing 258 tests (i.e. methods with the marked with the annotation *@Test*). These tests contain a total of 1,943 individual assertions. To measure code coverage of our unit tests we use EclEmma[5], a lightweight analysis tool available for the Eclipse development environment, which counts the number of lines that are executed (or not) when a suite of unit tests are executed. While this approach provides only a rough approximation of how well the unit tests "cover" the source code, we have found anecdotally that code with higher coverage reported by EclEmma proves to be more reliable and easier to maintain. Overall, our test suite provides 74.3% code coverage of ClearTK (5,391 lines covered out of 7,252) after factoring out automatically generated code created by JCasGen. Much of the uncovered code corresponds to the blocks catching rare exceptions. While it is important to test that code throws exceptions when it is expected to, forcing test code to throw all exceptions that are explicitly caught can be tedious and sometimes technically quite difficult.

5 Discussion

We learned several lessons while building our test suite. We started writing tests using Groovy, a dynamic language for the Java Virtual Machine. The hope was to simplify testing by using a less verbose language than Java. While Groovy provides a great syntax for creating tests that are much less verbose, we found that creating and maintaining these unit tests was cumbersome using the Eclipse plug-in that was available at the time (Summer 2007). In particular, refactoring tasks such as changing class names or method names would succeed in the Java code, but the Groovy test code would not be updated, a similar problem to that of UIMA's XML descriptor files. We also found that Eclipse became less responsive because user actions would often wait for the Groovy compiler to

[4] http://junit.org
[5] http://www.eclemma.org

complete. Additionally, Groovy tests involving Java's Generics would sometimes work on one platform (Windows) and fail on another (Linux or Mac). For these reasons we abandoned using Groovy and converted our tests to Java. It should be noted that the authors are novice users of Groovy and that Groovy (and the Eclipse Groovy plug-in) may have matured significantly in the intervening two years.

Another challenge we confronted while building our test suite was the use of licensed data. For example, ClearTK contains a component for reading and parsing PennTreebank formatted data. One of our tests reads in and parses the entire PennTreebank corpus, but since we do not have the rights to redistribute the PennTreeBank, we could not include this test as part of the test suite distributed with ClearTK. So as not to lose this valuable test, we created a sibling project of ClearTK which is not publicly available, but from which we could run tests on ClearTK. This sibling project now contains all of our unit tests which use data we cannot distribute. We are considering making this project available separately for those who have access to the relevant data sets.

We have begun to compile a growing list of best practices for our test suite. These include:

Reuse JCas objects. In UIMA, creating a JCas object is expensive. Instead of creating a new JCas object for each test, a single JCas object should be reused for many tests where possible.

Refer to descriptors by name, not location. UIMA allows descriptors to be located by either "location" (a file system path) or "name" (a Java-style dotted package name). Descriptors referred to by "name" can be found in a .jar file, while descriptors referred to by "location" cannot. This applies to imports of both type system descriptions (e.g. in component descriptors) and to imports of CAS processors (e.g. in collection processing engine descriptors).

Test loading of descriptor files. As discussed, XML descriptor files can become stale in an evolving codebase. Simply loading each descriptor in UIMA and verifying that the parameters are as expected is often enough to keep the descriptor files working if the actual component code is being properly checked through other tests.

Test copyright and license statements. We found it useful to add unit tests that search through our source files (both Java code and descriptor files) and verify that appropriate copyright and license statements are present. Such statements were a requirement of the technology transfer office we were working with, and were often accidentally omitted when new source files were added to ClearTK. Adding a unit test to check for this meant that we caught such omissions much earlier.

As ClearTK has grown in size and complexity its test suite has proven many times over to be a vital instrument in detecting bugs introduced by extending or refactoring existing code. We have found that the code in UUTUC has greatly decreased the burden of maintaining and extending this test suite, and so we have made it available for others to use.

References

Philip V. Ogren, Philipp G. Wetzler, and Steven Bethard. 2008. ClearTK: a UIMA toolkit for statistical natural language processing. In UIMA for NLP workshop at LREC.

David Ferrucci and Adam Lally. 2004. UIMA: an architectural approach to unstructured information processing in the corporate research environment. Natural Language Engineering, 10(3-4):327–348.

Context-Dependent Regression Testing for Natural Language Processing

Elaine Farrow
Human Communication Research Centre
School of Informatics
University of Edinburgh
Edinburgh, UK
Elaine.Farrow@ed.ac.uk

Myroslava O. Dzikovska
Human Communication Research Centre
School of Informatics
University of Edinburgh
Edinburgh, UK
M.Dzikovska@ed.ac.uk

Abstract

Regression testing of natural language systems is problematic for two main reasons: component input and output is complex, and system behaviour is context-dependent. We have developed a generic approach which solves both of these issues. We describe our regression tool, CONTEST, which supports context-dependent testing of dialogue system components, and discuss the regression test sets we developed, designed to effectively isolate components from changes and problems earlier in the pipeline. We believe that the same approach can be used in regression testing for other dialogue systems, as well as in testing any complex NLP system containing multiple components.

1 Introduction

Natural language processing systems, and dialogue systems in particular, often consist of large sets of components operating as a pipeline, including parsing, semantic interpretation, dialogue management, planning, and generation. Testing such a system can be a difficult task for several reasons. First, the component output may be context-dependent. This is particularly true for a dialogue system – reference resolution, ellipsis, and sometimes generation typically have to query the system state to produce their output, which depends both on the state of the world (propositions defined in a knowledge base) and on the dialogue history (object salience). Under these conditions, unit testing using the input and output of a single component in isolation is of limited value – the entire system state needs to be preserved to check that context-dependent components are functioning as expected.

Second, the inputs and outputs of most system components are usually very complex and often change over time as the system develops. When two complex representations are compared it may be difficult to determine what impact any change is likely to have on system performance (far-reaching or relatively trivial). Further, if we test components in isolation by saving their inputs, and these inputs are reasonably complex, then it will become difficult to maintain the test sets for the components further along the pipeline (such as diagnosis and generation) as the output of the earlier components changes during development.

The simplest way to deal with both of these issues would be to save a set of test dialogues as a gold standard, checking that the final system output is correct given the system input. However, this presents another problem. If a single component (generation, for example) malfunctions, it becomes impossible to verify that a component earlier in the pipeline (for example, reference resolution) is working properly. In principle we could also save the messages passing between components and compare their content, but then we are faced again with the problems arising from the complexity of component input and output which we described above.

To solve these problems, we developed a regression tool called CONTEST (for CONtext-dependent TESTing). CONTEST allows the authors of individual system components to control what information to record for regression testing. Test dialogues are

Proceedings of the NAACL HLT Workshop on Software Engineering, Testing, and Quality Assurance for Natural Language Processing, pages 5–13,
Boulder, Colorado, June 2009. ©2009 Association for Computational Linguistics

saved and replayed through the system, and individual components are tested by comparing only their specific regression output, ignoring the outputs generated by other components. The components are isolated by maintaining a minimal set of inputs that are guaranteed to be processed correctly.

To deal with issues of output complexity we extend the approach of de Paiva and King (2008) for testing a deep parser. They created test sets at different levels of granularity, some including detailed representations, but some just saving very simple output of a textual entailment component. They showed that, given a carefully selected test set, testing on the final system output can be a fast and effective way to discover problems in the interpretation pipeline.

We show how the same idea can be used to test other dialogue system components as well. We describe the design of three different test sets that effectively isolate the interpretation, tutorial planning and generation components of our system. Using CONTEST allows us to detect system errors and maintain consistent test sets even as the underlying representations change, and gives us much greater confidence that the results of our testing are relevant to the performance of the system with real users.

The rest of this paper is organised as follows. In Section 2 we describe our system and its components in more detail. The design of the CONTEST tool and the test sets are described in Sections 3 and 4. Finally, in Section 5 we discuss how the interactive nature of the dialogue influences the design of the test sets and the process of verifying the answers; and we discuss features that we would like to implement in the future.

2 Background

This work has been carried out to support the development of BEETLE (Callaway et al., 2007), a tutorial dialogue system for basic electricity and electronics. The goal of the BEETLE system is to teach conceptual knowledge using natural language dialogue. Students interact with the system through a graphical user interface (GUI) which includes a chat interface,[1] a window to browse through slides containing reading material and diagrams, and an interface to a circuit simulator where students can build and manipulate circuits.

The system consists of twelve components altogether, including a knowledge base representing the state of the world, a curriculum planner responsible for the lesson structure, and dialogue management and NLP components. We developed CONTEST so that it could be used to test any system component, though our testing focuses on the natural language understanding and generation components.[2]

BEETLE uses a standard natural language processing pipeline, starting with a parser, lexical interpreter, and dialogue manager. The dialogue manager handles all input from the GUI (text, button presses and circuits) and also supports generic dialogue processing, such as dealing with interpretation failures and moving the lesson along. Student answers are processed by the diagnosis and tutorial planning components (discussed below), which function similarly to planning and execution components in task oriented dialogue systems. Finally, a generation subsystem converts the semantic representations output by the tutorial planner into the final text to be presented to the student.

The components communicate with each other using the Open Agent Architecture (Martin et al., 1998). CONTEST is implemented as an OAA agent, accepting requests to record messages. However, OAA is not essential for the system design – any communication architecture which supports adding extra agents into a system would work equally well.

BEETLE aims to get students to support their reasoning using natural language, since explanations and contentful talk are associated with learning gain (Purandare and Litman, 2008). This requires detailed analyses of student answers in terms of correct, incorrect and missing parts (Dzikovska et al., 2008; Nielsen et al., 2008). Thus, we use the TRIPS parser (Allen et al., 2007), a deep parser which produces detailed analyses of student input. The lexical interpreter extracts a list of objects and relationships mentioned, which are checked against the expected answer. These lists are fairly long – many expected answers have ten or more relations in them. The

[1]The student input is currently typed to avoid issues with automated speech recognition of complex utterances.

[2]All our components are rule-based, but we expect the same approach would work for components of a statistical nature.

diagnoser categorises each of the objects and relationships as correct, contradictory or irrelevant. The tutorial planner makes decisions about the remediation strategy, choosing one strategy from a set of about thirteen depending on the question type and tutorial context. Finally, the generation system uses the FUF/SURGE (Elhadad, 1991) deep generator to generate feedback automatically.

Obviously, the output from the deep parser and the input to the tutorial planner and generator are quite complex, giving rise to the types of problems that we discussed in the introduction. We already had a tool for unit-testing the parser output (Swift et al., 2004), plus some separate tools to test the diagnoser and the generation component, but the complexity of the representations made it impractical to maintain large test sets that depended on such complex inputs and outputs. We also wanted a unified way to test all the components in the context of the entire system. This led to the creation of CONTEST, which we describe in the rest of the paper.

3 The CONTEST Tool

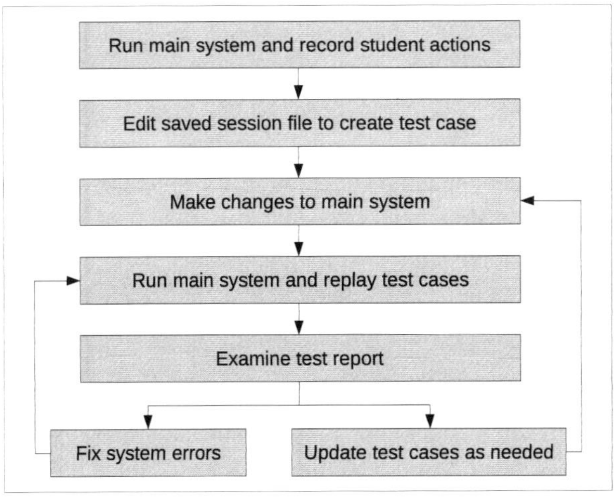

Figure 1: The regression testing process.

In this section we describe the process for creating and using test cases, illustrated in Figure 1. The first step in building a useful regression tool is to make it possible to run the same dialogue through the system many times without retyping the student answers. We added a wrapper around the GUI to intercept and record the user actions and system calls for later playback, thus creating a complete record of the session. Every time our system runs, a new saved session file is automatically created and saved in a standard location. This file forms the basis for our test cases. It uses an XML format, which is human-readable and hand-editable, easily extensible and amenable to automatic processing. A (slightly simplified) example of a saved session file is shown in Figure 2. Here we can see that a slide was displayed, the tutor asked the question "Which components (if any) are in a closed path in circuit 1?" and the student answered "the battery and the lightbulb".

Creating a new test case is then a simple matter of starting the system and performing the desired actions, such as entering text and building circuits in the circuit simulator. If the system is behaving as it should, the saved session file can be used directly as a test case. If the system output is not as desired, the file can be edited in any text editor.

Of course, this only allows the final output of the system to be tested, and we have already discussed the shortcomings of such an approach: if a component late in the pipeline has problems, there is no way to tell if earlier components behaved as expected. To remedy this, we added a mechanism for components other than the GUI to record their own information in the saved session file.

Components can be tested in effective isolation by combining two mechanisms: carefully designed test sets which focus on a single component and (importantly) are expected to succeed even if some other component is having problems; and a regression tool which allows us to test the output of an individual component. Our test sets are discussed in detail in Section 4. The remainder of this section describes the design of the tool.

CONTEST reads in a saved session file and reproduces the user actions (such as typing answers or building circuits), producing a new saved session file as its output. If there have been changes to the system since the test was created, replaying the same actions may lead to new slides and tutor messages being displayed, and different recorded output from intermediate components. For example, given the same student answers, the diagnosis may have changed, leading to different tutor feedback. We compare the newly generated output file against the input file. If there are no differences, the test is considered to have passed. As the input and output files

```
<test>
  <action agent="tutor" method="showSlide">
    lesson1-oe/exercise/img1.html
  </action>
  <action agent="tutor" method="showOutput">
    Which components (if any) are in a closed path in circuit 1?
  </action>
  <action agent="student" method="submitText">
    the battery and the lightbulb
  </action>
</test>
```

Figure 2: A saved session file showing a single interaction between tutor and student.

are identical in format, the comparison can be done using a 'diff' command.

With each component recording its own output, it can be the case that there are many differences between old and new files. It is therefore important to be able to choose the level of detail we want when comparing saved session files, so that the output of a single component can be checked independently of other system behaviour. We solved this problem by creating a set of standard XSLT filters. One filter picks out just the dialogue between student and tutor to produce a transcript of the session. Other filters select the output from one particular component, for example the tutorial planner, with the tutor questions included to provide context. In general, we wrote one filter for each component.

CONTEST creates a test report by comparing the expected and actual outputs of the system on each test run. We specify which filter to use (based on which component we are testing). If the test fails, we can examine the relevant differences using the 'ediff' mode in the emacs text editor. More sophisticated approaches are possible, such as using a further XSL transform to count all the errors of a particular type, but we have found ediff to be good enough for our purposes. With the filters in place we only see the differences for the component we are testing. Since component regression output is designed to be small and human-readable, checking the differences is a very quick process.

Test cases can be run individually or in groups.[3] Using CONTEST, we can create a single report for a group of test cases: the individual outputs are combined to create a new output file for the group and this is compared to the (combined) input file, with filters applied in the usual way. This is a very useful feature, allowing us to create a report for all the 'good answer' cases (for example) in one step.

Differences do not always indicate errors; sometimes they are simply changes or additions to the recorded information. After satisfying ourselves that the reported differences are intentional changes, we can update the test cases to reflect the output of the latest run. Subsequent runs will test against the new behaviour. CONTEST includes an update tool which can update a group of cases with a single command. This is simpler and less error-prone than editing potentially hundreds of files by hand.

4 Test Cases

We have built several test sets for each component, amounting to more than 400 individual test cases. We describe examples of the test sets for three of our components in more detail below, to demonstrate how we use CONTEST.

4.1 Interpretation Test Cases

We have a test set consisting of 'good answers' for each of the questions in our system which we use to test the interpretation component. The regression information recorded by the interpretation component includes the internal ID code of the matched answer and a code indicating whether it is a 'best', 'good' or 'minimal' answer. This is enough to allow us to de-

[3]Test cases are usually grouped by directory, but symbolic links allow us to use the same case in several groups.

```
<test name="closed_path_discussion">
  <action agent="tutor" method="showOutput">
    What are the conditions that are required to make a bulb light up?
  </action>
  <action agent="student" method="submitText">
    a bulb must be in a closed path with the battery
  </action>
  <action agent="simpleDiagnosis" method="logForRegression">
    student-act: answer atype: diagnosis consistency: []
    code: complete subcode: best
    answer_id: conditions_for_bulb_to_light_ans1
  </action>
</test>
```

Figure 3: A sample test case from our 'good answers' set showing the diagnosis produced for the student's answer.

tect many possible errors in interpretation. We can run this test set after every change to the parsing or interpretation components.

A (slightly simplified) example of our XML test case format is shown in Figure 3, with the tutor question "What are the conditions that are required to make a bulb light up?" and the student answer "a bulb must be in a closed path with the battery". The answer diagnosis shows that the system recognised that the student was attempting to answer the question (rather than asking for help), that the answer match was complete, with no missing or incorrect parts, and the answer was consistent with the state of the world as perceived by the system.[4] The matched answer is marked as the best one for that question.

While the recorded information does not supply the full interpretation, it can suggest the source of various possible errors. If interpretation fails, the student act will be set to `uninterpretable`, and the `code` will correspond to the reason for failed interpretation: `unknown_input` if the parse failed, `unknown_mapping` or `restriction_failure` if lexical interpretation failed, and `unresolvable` if reference resolution failed. If interpretation worked, but took incorrect scoping or attachment decisions, the resulting proposition is likely to be inconsistent with the current knowledge base, and an inconsistency code will be reported. In addition, verifying the matched answer ID provides some information in case only a partial interpretation was produced. Sometimes different answer IDs correspond to answers that are very complete versus answers that are acceptable because they address the key point of the question, but miss some small details. Thus if a different answer ID has matched, it indicates that some information was probably lost in interpretation.

The codes we report were not devised specifically for the regression tests. They are used internally to allow the system to produce accurate feedback about misunderstandings. However, because they indicate where the error is likely to originate (parsing, lexical interpretation, scoping and disambiguation), they can help us to track it down.

We have another test set for 'special cases', such as the student requesting a hint or giving up. An example is shown in Figure 4. Here the student gives up completely on the first question, then asks for help with the second. We use this test case to check that the set phrases "I give up" and "help" are understood by the system. The 'special cases' test set includes a variety of help request phrasings observed in the corpora we collected. Note that this example was recorded while using a tutorial policy that responds to help requests by simply providing the answer. This does not matter for testing interpretation, since the information recorded in the test case will distinguish help requests from give ups, regardless

[4]Sometimes students are unable to interpret diagrams, or are lacking essential background knowledge, and therefore say things that contradict the information in the domain model. The system detects and remediates such cases differently from general errors in explanations (Dzikovska et al., 2006).

T: Which components (if any) are in a closed path in circuit 1?
S: I give up
T: The answer is the battery and the bulb in 1.
T: Which components (if any) are in a closed path in circuit 2?
S: help
T: Here's the answer. The bulb in 2.

Figure 4: The transcript of a test case for "I give up" and "help". **T:** is the tutor, **S:** is the student.

of the specific tutorial policy used by the system.

Finally, we have a test set for detection of uninterpretable utterances. In a tutoring system, students often use incorrect terminology or unexpected phrasings which the system cannot understand. While we expect coverage and robustness of parsing and interpretation components to improve as the system develops, some percentage of errors is to be expected simply because even state-of-the-art parsers are not 100% accurate. Thus the system needs to detect problems whenever possible, and produce useful help messages. We have collected a set of student utterances that correspond to typical interpretation problems – failed parses, unknown words, sentences that are parsed but the parser makes an incorrect attachment decision, sentences where the student used terminology incorrectly (violating sortal constraints encoded in the knowledge base), a pronominal referent that could not be resolved. Identifying the problem type correctly is important because it affects later processing in the dialogue manager and tutorial planner. Thus we have a set of test cases using the collected sentences, which we use to ensure that the problems are flagged correctly.

4.2 Tutoring Test Cases

The BEETLE tutorial planner makes decisions on system behaviour and corresponds to planning and execution components in other dialogue systems. Here, we are attempting to test that the tutorial planner selected the right system action. Therefore, since we are not testing the interpretation component, we don't vary the form of the language we use. Instead, we vary the combination of good and bad student answers, and record the action chosen by the system.

T: Predict the state (on, off) of each bulb in diagram 1.
S: all bulbs are off
T: OK, we'll check your prediction in a moment.
T: Predict the state (on, off) of each bulb in diagram 2.
S: all bulbs are off
T: OK, we'll check your prediction in a moment.
T: Test your prediction for diagram 1 by opening both switches and observing the bulbs.
T: Test your prediction for diagram 2 by closing both switches and observing the bulbs.
T: Did the bulbs behave the way you expected?
S: no
T: Right. In your second prediction, you said that Bulb A, Bulb B and Bulb C would be off. But Bulb A, Bulb B and Bulb C are lit.

Figure 5: A tutorial planner test case transcript. **T:** is the tutor, **S:** is the student.

The tutorial planner chooses feedback in 2 stages. First, a general algorithm is chosen depending on the exercise type and student input type: there are separate algorithms for addressing, for example, what to do if the student input was not interpreted, and for correct and incorrect answers. Choosing the algorithm requires some computation depending on the question context. Once the main algorithm is chosen, different tutorial strategies can be selected, and this is reflected in the regression output: the system records a keyword corresponding to the chosen algorithm, and then the name of the strategy along with key strategy parameters.

For example, Figure 5 shows the transcript from a test case for a common exercise type from our lessons: a so called predict-verify-evaluate sequence. In this example, the student is asked to predict the behaviour of three light bulbs in a circuit, test it by manipulating the circuit in the simulation environment, and then evaluate whether their predictions matched the circuit behaviour. The system reinforces the point of the exercise by producing a summary of discrepancies between the student's

```
<action agent="tutor" method="showOutput">
  Did the bulbs behave the way you expected?
</action>
<action agent="student" method="submitText">
  no
</action>
<action agent="tc-bee" method="logForRegression">
  EVALUATE (INCORRECT-PREDICTION NO_NO)
</action>
```

Figure 6: An excerpt from a tutorial planner test case showing the recorded summary output.

predictions and the observed outcomes.

An excerpt from the corresponding test case is shown in Figure 6. Here we can see the tutor ask the evaluation question "Did the bulbs behave the way you expected?" and the student answer "no". The `EVALUATE` algorithm was chosen to handle the student answer, and from the set of available strategies the `INCORRECT-PREDICTION` strategy was chosen. That strategy takes a parameter indicating if there was a discrepancy when the student evaluated the results (here `NO_NO`, corresponding to the expected and actual evaluation result inputs).

In contrast, in the first example in Figure 4, where the student gives up and doesn't provide an answer, the tutorial planner output is `REMEDIATE (BOTTOM-OUT Q_IDENTIFY)`. This shows that the system has chosen to use a `REMEDIATE` algorithm, and a 'bottom-out' (giving away the answer) strategy for remediation. The strategy parameter `Q_IDENTIFY` (which depends on the question type) determines the phrasing to be used in the generator to verbalise the tutor's feedback.

The saved output allows us to see that the correct algorithm was chosen to handle the student input (for example, that the `REMEDIATE` algorithm is correctly chosen after an incorrect student answer to an explanation question), and that the algorithm chooses a strategy appropriate for the tutorial context. Certain errors can still go undetected here, for example, if the algorithm for verbalising the chosen strategy in the generator is broken. Developing summary inputs to detect such errors is part of planned future work.

In order to isolate the tutorial planner from interpretation, we use standard fixed phrasings for student answers. The answer phrasings in the 'good answers' test set for interpretation (described in Section 4.1) are guaranteed to be understood correctly, so we use only these phrasings in our tutorial planner test cases. Thus, we are able to construct tests which will not be affected by problems in the interpretation pipeline.

4.3 Generation Test Cases

To test generation, we have a set of test cases where the student immediately says "I give up" in response to each question. This phrase is used in our system to prevent the students getting stuck – the tutorial policy is to immediately stop and give the answer to the question. The answers given are generated by a deep generator from internal semantic representations, so this test set gives us the assurance that all relevant domain content is being generated properly. This is not a complete test for the generation capabilities of our system, since each explanation question can have several possible answers of varying degrees of quality (suggested by experienced human tutors (Dzikovska et al., 2008)), and we always choose the best possible answer when the student gives up. However, it gives us confidence that the student can give up at any point and receive an answer which can be used as a template for future answers.

5 Discussion and Future Work

We have created more than 400 individual test cases so far. There are more than 50 for the interpretation component, more than 150 for the tutorial planner and more than 200 for the generation component. We are developing new test sets based on other scenarios, such as responding to each question with a help request. We are also refining the summary information recorded by each component.

An important feature of our testing approach is the use of short summaries rather than the internal representations of component inputs and outputs. Well-designed summaries provide key information in an easy-to-read format that can remain constant as internal formats change and develop over time. We believe that this approach would be useful for other language processing systems, since at present there are few standardised formats in the community and representations are typically developed and refined together with the algorithms that use them.

The decision about what information to include in the summary is vital to the success and overall usefulness of the regression tool. If too much detail is recorded, there will be many spurious changes and it will be burdensome to keep a large regression set updated. If too little detail is recorded, unwanted changes in the system may go undetected. The content of the test cases we discussed in Section 4 represents our approach to such decisions.

Interpretation was perhaps the most difficult, because it has a particularly complex output. In determining the information to record, we were following the solution of de Paiva and King (2008) who use the decision result of the textual entailment system as a way to efficiently test parser output. For our system, the information output by the diagnoser about answer correctness proved to have a similar function – it effectively provides information about whether the output of the interpretation component was usable, without the need to check details carefully.

The main challenge for our tutorial planner and generation components (corresponding to planning and execution components in a task-oriented dialogue system) was to ensure that they were sufficiently isolated so as to be unaffected by errors in interpretation. We achieve this by maintaining a small set of known phrasings which are guaranteed to be interpreted correctly; this ensures that in practice, the downstream components are isolated from unwanted changes in interpretation.

Our overall methodology of recording and testing summary information for individual components can be used with any complex NLP system. The specific details of what information to record obviously depends on the domain, but our experience suggests some general principles. For testing the interpretation pipeline, it is useful to record pre-existing error codes and a qualitative summary of the information used to decide on the next system action. Where we record the code output by the diagnoser, an information seeking system could record, for example, the number of slots filled and the number of items retrieved from a database. It is also useful to record decisions taken by the system, or actions performed in response to user input; so, just as we record information about the chosen tutorial policy, other systems can record the action taken – whether it is to search the database, query a new slot, or confirm a slot value.

One major improvement that we have planned for the future is adding another layer of test case management to CONTEST, to enable us to produce summaries and statistics about the total number of test cases that have passed and failed, instead of checking reports individually. Such statistics can be implemented easily using another XSL transform on top of the existing filters to count the number of test cases with no differences and produce summary counts of each type of error detected.

6 Conclusion

The regression tool we developed, CONTEST, solves two of the major issues faced when testing dialogue systems: context-dependence of component behaviour and complexity of component output. We developed a generic approach based on running saved dialogues through the system, and checking summary information recorded by different components against separate gold standards. We demonstrated that test sets can be designed in such a way as to effectively isolate downstream components from changes and problems earlier in the pipeline. We believe that the same approach can be used in regression testing for other dialogue systems, as well as in testing any complex NLP system containing multiple components.

Acknowledgements

This work has been supported in part by Office of Naval Research grant N000140810043. We thank Charles Callaway for help with generation and tutoring tests.

References

James Allen, Myroslava Dzikovska, Mehdi Manshadi, and Mary Swift. 2007. Deep linguistic processing for spoken dialogue systems. In *Proceedings of the ACL-07 Workshop on Deep Linguistic Processing*.

Charles B. Callaway, Myroslava Dzikovska, Elaine Farrow, Manuel Marques-Pita, Colin Matheson, and Johanna D. Moore. 2007. The Beetle and BeeDiff tutoring systems. In *Proceedings of the SLaTE-2007 Workshop*, Farmington, Pennsylvania, USA, September.

Valeria de Paiva and Tracy Holloway King. 2008. Designing testsuites for grammar-based systems in applications. In *Coling 2008: Proceedings of the workshop on Grammar Engineering Across Frameworks*, pages 49–56, Manchester, England, August. Coling 2008 Organizing Committee.

Myroslava O. Dzikovska, Charles B. Callaway, and Elaine Farrow. 2006. Interpretation and generation in a knowledge-based tutorial system. In *Proceedings of EACL-06 workshop on knowledge and reasoning for language processing*, Trento, Italy, April.

Myroslava O. Dzikovska, Gwendolyn E. Campbell, Charles B. Callaway, Natalie B. Steinhauser, Elaine Farrow, Johanna D. Moore, Leslie A. Butler, and Colin Matheson. 2008. Diagnosing natural language answers to support adaptive tutoring. In *Proceedings 21st International FLAIRS Conference*, Coconut Grove, Florida, May.

Michael Elhadad. 1991. FUF: The universal unifier user manual version 5.0. Technical Report CUCS-038-91, Dept. of Computer Science, Columbia University.

D. Martin, A. Cheyer, and D. Moran. 1998. Building distributed software systems with the open agent architecture. In *Proceedings of the Third International Conference on the Practical Application of Intelligent Agents and Multi-Agent Technology*, Blackpool, Lancashire, UK.

Rodney D. Nielsen, Wayne Ward, and James H. Martin. 2008. Learning to assess low-level conceptual understanding. In *Proceedings 21st International FLAIRS Conference*, Coconut Grove, Florida, May.

Amruta Purandare and Diane Litman. 2008. Content-learning correlations in spoken tutoring dialogs at word, turn and discourse levels. In *Proceedings 21st International FLAIRS Conference*, Coconut Grove, Florida, May.

Mary D. Swift, Joel Tetreault, and Myroslava O. Dzikovska. 2004. Semi-automatic syntactic and semantic corpus annotation with a deep parser. In *Proceedings of LREC-2004*.

Using Paraphrases of Deep Semantic Representions to Support Regression Testing in Spoken Dialogue Systems

Beth Ann Hockey
UC Santa Cruz and BAHRC LLC
Mail Stop 19-26, UCSC UARC
NASA Ames Research Center, Moffett Field, CA 94035–1000
bahockey@bahrc.net

Manny Rayner
University of Geneva, TIM/ISSCO
40 bvd du Pont-d'Arve, CH-1211 Geneva 4, Switzerland
Emmanuel.Rayner@unige.ch

Abstract

Rule-based spoken dialogue systems require a good regression testing framework if they are to be maintainable. We argue that there is a tension between two extreme positions when constructing the database of test examples. On the one hand, if the examples consist of input/output tuples representing many levels of internal processing, they are fine-grained enough to catch most processing errors, but unstable under most system modifications. If the examples are pairs of user input and final system output, they are much more stable, but too coarse-grained to catch many errors. In either case, there are fairly severe difficulties in judging examples correctly. We claim that a good compromise can be reached by implementing a paraphrasing mechanism which maps internal semantic representations into surface forms, and carrying out regression testing using paraphrases of semantic forms rather than the semantic forms themselves. We describe an implementation of the idea using the Open Source Regulus toolkit, where paraphrases are produced using Regulus grammars compiled in generation mode. Paraphrases can also be used at runtime to produce confirmations. By compiling the paraphrase grammar a second time, as a recogniser, it is possible in a simple and natural way to guarantee that confirmations are always within system coverage.

1 Introduction

Design features that enable important functionality in medium vocabulary, mixed-initiative spoken dialogue systems also create challenges for the project cycle, and in particular for regression testing. Two issues that make regression testing particularly difficult are the need for context dependent interpretation, and the use of multiple levels of representation. Both of these features are typically necessary for non-trivial dialogue systems of this type. Multiple levels of processing, as usual, provide necessary modularity. Context dependent interpretation enables responses that are tuned to the current circumstances of the interaction or the world, and frequently helps resolve ambiguity.

The implications for regression testing, though, are less happy. The context of each interaction in the test suite needs to be stored as part of the interaction. Multiple levels of representation that are, for example, useful for doing ellipsis resolution or reference resolution, also complicate testing. If regression testing is done on each separate level of processing, or involves internal representations, small changes to a representation at one level can mean having to revise and rejudge the entire test suite to keep it up to date.

This paper discusses the methodology we have developed to address regression testing issues within the Regulus framework. Regulus (Rayner et al., 2006) is an Open Source toolkit for builting medium

Proceedings of the NAACL HLT Workshop on Software Engineering, Testing, and Quality Assurance for Natural Language Processing, pages 14–21,
Boulder, Colorado, June 2009. ©2009 Association for Computational Linguistics

vocabulary spoken dialogue and translation applications, and has been used to build a number of non-trivial spoken dialogue systems. Prominent examples include NASA's Clarissa Procedure Navigator (Rayner et al., 2005), Geneva University's multi-modal mobile-platform Calendar application (Tsourakis et al., 2008), SDS, a prototype in-car system developed by UC Santa Cruz in collaboration with Ford Motors Research which was voted first in Ford's 2007 internal technology fair, and Taxi, a speech-enabled game in which the user interacts with a simulated cab driver to navigate around a map of Manhattan. It has also been used to build the MedSLT medical speech translation system (Bouillon et al., 2008).

The Regulus platform includes tools for developing feature grammars, and compiling them in various ways. In particular, it is possible to compile grammars into generators, and use them to support paraphrasing from the internal semantic representations created during dialogue processing. This capability is key to the newest part of our regression testing approach, and is discussed in detail in Section 3. First, though, Section 2 gives an overview of Regulus and the architecture of Regulus-based systems; we discuss features that complicate regression testing, and how to address these problems within this type of architecture. Section 4 discusses how test suites are constructed and what types of items they may contain. In Section 5 we show how paraphrases can also be included in the run-time architecture. The final section concludes.

2 The Regulus platform

Regulus is an Open Source toolkit for building medium vocabulary grammar-based spoken dialogue and translation systems. The central idea is to base run-time processing on efficient, task-specific grammars derived from general, reusable, domain-independent core grammars. Early versions of Regulus used a single core grammar per language; a detailed description of the core grammar for English can be found in (Rayner et al., 2006, Chapter 9). More recently, there have been attempts to go further, and merge together core grammars for closely related languages (Bouillon et al., 2007).

The core grammars are automatically specialised,

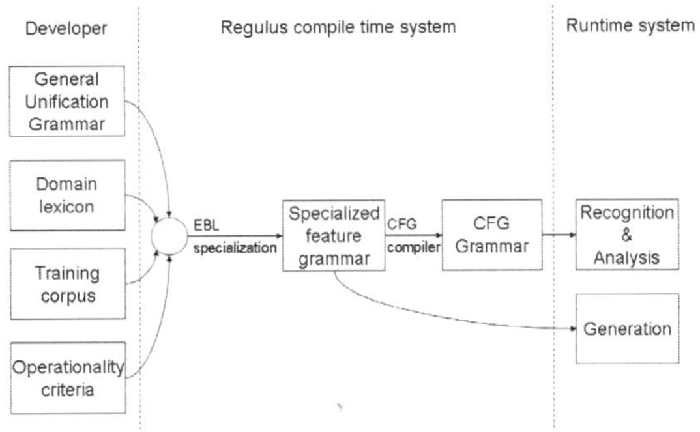

Figure 1: The Regulus compilation path. The general unification grammar is first transformed into a specialised feature grammar. This can then be transformed either into a CFG grammar and Nuance recogniser, or into a generator. and a Nuance recogniser.

using corpus-driven methods based on small corpora, to derive simpler grammars. Specialisation is both with respect to task (recognition, analysis, generation) and to application domain. The specialisation process uses the Explanation Based Learning algorithm (van Harmelen and Bundy, 1988; Rayner, 1988). It starts with a parsed treebank derived from the training corpus, and then divides the parse tree created from each training example into a set of one or more subtrees, following a set of domain- and grammar-specific rules conventionally known in the Machine Learning literature as operationality criteria. The rules in each subtree are then combined, using the unification operation, into a single rule. The set of all such rules constitutes a specialised unification grammar. Each of these specialised unification grammars is then subjected to a second compilation step, which converts it into its executable form. For analysis and generation, this form is a standard parser or generator. For recognition, it is a semantically annotated CFG grammar in the form required by the Nuance engine, which is then subjected to further Nuance-specific compilation steps to derive a speech recognition package. Figure 1 summarises compile-time processing.

The Regulus platform also contains infrastructure to support construction of applications which use the recognisers, parsers and generators as components. In this paper, we will only discuss spoken dialogue system applications. (There is also an elaborate infrastructure to support speech translation systems).

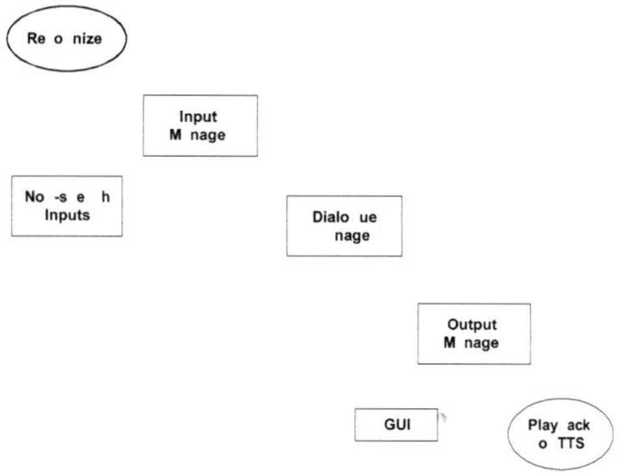
Re o nize
Input
M nage
No -s e h
Inputs
Dialo ue
nage
Output
M nage
GUI
Play ack
o TTS

sible to construct a regression test suite consisting of 4-tuples of the form

$$\langle InState, Move, OutState, Actions \rangle$$

There are however several problems. First, processing consists of much more than just the update function. It is optimistic to assume that the speech recogniser will be able to produce dialogue moves directly. In simple cases, this may be possible. In more complex cases, extra levels of processing become necessary; in other words, the IM component will generally have a substantial amount of structure.

There are several reasons for this. The representation delivered by the grammar-based speech recogniser is syntax-oriented; it needs to be translated into a semantic form. Again, because of context-dependency, this translation often needs to be carried out in more than one step. For example, in the Calendar application, a question like "When is the next meeting in Switzerland?" might be followed by the elliptical utterance "In England?". Some kind of mechanism is needed in order to resolve this to a representation meaning "When is the next meeting in England?" A separate mechanism is used to perform reference resolution. For instance, the default database for the Calendar application contains one person called "Nikos" and two called "Marianne". The question "Is Nikos attending the meeting?" needs to be converted into a database query that looks up the appropriate record; however, the structurally similar query "Is Marianne attending the meeting?" should produce a disambiguation query. Examples like these motivate the introduction of yet another processing step, which carries out reference resolution.

Of course, different systems will address these issues in different ways; but, whatever the solution, the general point remains that there will usually be many layers of representation. From a system development point of view, the problem is how to structure the regression testing needed in order to maintain the stability of each processing step. The most cautious and direct way to do this is to have a corpus of input/output tuples representing each individual step, but experience shows that this type of solution places an enormous burden on the annotators who are required to judge the correctness or otherwise of the tuples. First of all, under this approach the annotators must be experts capable of reading and understanding internal representations. Second, even very small changes in the system often require complete reannotation of the test corpus; for example, some data structure may have been changed so as to include an extra field. If constant rejudging is required to keep the test suite coherent with the current version of the system, either the testing is abandoned as overly difficult and time consuming, or it is done in a less careful way in order to speed up the process. Neither outcome is satisfactory.

If annotation uses input/output tuples referring to internal representations, the problems we have just named appear inescapable. At the opposite end of the spectrum, a common approach is not to look at internal representations at all, but only at input/output pairs consisting of top-level inputs and outputs. For example, we can pair "When is the next meeting in Geneva?" with "March 31 2009", and "Is Marianne attending the meeting?" with "Which Marianne do you mean?" This is generally, in practice, easier than doing regression testing on internal representations; the key advantages are that, since we are only dealing with pre-theoretical notions, annotation can be performed by non-experts, and annotations remain stable across most changes to internal representations.

Unfortunately, however, new problems arise. First, determining the correct output response for a given input is often tedious and slow. For example, in the Calendar application, this generally involves carrying out a database search. Suitable annotation tools can alleviate the pain here, but then a worse problem arises; it is often possible to produce a correct system response, even if processing is incorrect. For instance, even if the system correctly answers "No" to a yes/no question, this proves very little; the question could have been interpreted in a multitude of ways, and still produced a negative answer. Knowing that a WH-question provides a correct answer says more, but can still often be misleading. Suppose, for example, that we know that the Calendar system correctly answers "None" to the question "What meetings are there during the next week?" and there are no meetings for the next 15 days. We will be unable to tell whether the question has been interpreted as "What meetings are there during the

World Context	time=2008-10-14 14:34, speaker=mike
Last Para	(none)
Input	when is the next meeting with mark
Paraphrase	when is [the next meeting attended by mark green]
World Context	time=2008-10-16 09:47, speaker=mike
Last Para	(none)
Input	when is my next meeting with mark
Paraphrase	when is [the next meeting attended by mark green and mike jones]
World Context	time=2007-07-08 15:03, speaker=susan
Last Para	(none)
Input	is there a meeting next week
Paraphrase	are there meetings between Mon Jul 9 2007 and Sun Jul 15 2007
World Context	time=2008-11-17 18:20, speaker=mike
Last Para	(none)
Input	do i have a meeting on friday morning this week
Paraphrase	are there meetings between 06:00 and 12:00 on Fri Nov 21 2008 attended by mike jones
World Context	time=2008-11-12 10:19, speaker=mike
Last Para	when is [the next meeting attended by mike jones]
Input	will alex participate
Paraphrase	will that meeting be attended by alex miller
World Context	time=2007-07-08 15:56), speaker=susan
Last Para	are there meetings on Mon Jul 9 2007
Input	how about on tuesday
Paraphrase	are there meetings on Tue Jul 10 2007

Table 1: Examples of regression testing tuples in the English Calendar system. Each tuple shows the current world context (timestamp and speaker), the preceding paraphrase, the input, and the paraphrase produced from it.

next 7 days?", as "What meetings are there during the 7 day period starting this Sunday?" or as "What meetings are there during the 7 day period starting this Monday?" Examples like these mean that regression testing often fails to catch bugs introduced by system changes.

3.2 Paraphrasing dialogue moves

To summarise: when carrying out regression testing, we have two competing requirements. First, we need to be able to access internal representations, since they are so informative. At the same time, we prefer to work with human-readable, pretheorically meaningful objects, which will be stable at least under most small changes in underlying representations. There is, in fact, a good compromise between these goals: we define a transformation which realises the dialogue move as a human-readable string, which we call a *dialogue move paraphrase*. So, for example, consider the possible interpretations when, on March 6 2009, a user asks "What meetings are there during the next week?". If "What meetings are there during the next week?" is interpreted as "What meetings are there during the next 7 days?", then the paraphrase might be "What meetings are there between Fri Mar 6 and Thu Mar 12 2009?"; if the interpretation is "What meetings are there during the 7 day period starting this Monday?", then the corresponding paraphrase would be "What meetings are there between Mon Mar 9 and Sun Mar 15 2009?" Regression testing can be carried out using paraphrases of dialogue moves, rather than the dialogue moves themselves.

The paraphrase mechanism is implemented as a Regulus grammar, compiled in generation mode, which directly relates a dialogue move and its surface form. We have found that it is not hard to design "paraphrase grammars" which produce outputs fulfilling the main design requirements. Regression testing is carried out on tuples consisting of the preceding paraphrase, the world context (if any), the input, and the resulting paraphrase. Examples of such tuples for the English Calendar grammar are shown in Table 1; in Calendar, the world context consists of the utterance time-stamp and the speaker.

A tuple combines the results of IM and DM (but not OM) processing for a given example, and presents them in a pre-theoretically meaningful way. Although they are not as fine-grained as tuples for individual processing steps, they are stable over most system changes. In the opposite direction, they are far more fine-grained than straight system input/system output tuples. They are much easier to judge than both of the other types of tuple. The bottom line, at least as far as we are concerned, is that a regression testing database of paraphrase-based tuples can actually be maintained without inordinate effort, implying corresponding gains for system stability. Previously, this was impossible.

The idea of creating paraphrases from dialogue moves is of course not new; in previous work, however, they have generally been used at runtime to provide feedback to the user as to how their input has been interpreted by the system. Although in the current discussion we have been more concerned with their use in regression testing, we have in fact also employed them for the more traditional purpose.

We return to this theme in Section 5. First, we describe in more detail where our test suites come from.

4 Collecting test suites

The tradition in the speech engineering community is that a test suite consists of a list of recorded wavfiles, together with accompanying transcriptions. The Nuance platform contains a fair amount of infrastructure, in particular the `batchrec` utility, for processing lists of wavfiles. These tools are very useful for computing measures like WER, and there is a strong temptation to try to build on top of them. After a while, however, we discovered that they meshed poorly with the the basic goals of regression testing in a spoken dialogue system, which revolve around speech *understanding* rather than speech *recognition*. There are two central problems. One of them is context-dependence, which we have already discussed at length. The other is the fact that many applications require that the IM process both speech and non-speech actions, with the sequence and even the timing of actions being important.

For example, as we have already seen, time is a central concept in the Calendar system. If the user says "Are there any meetings this afternoon?" the system interprets her as meaning "Are there any meetings from now until the end of the afternoon?" This means that the exact clock time for each utterance is important. In the Taxi application, the taxi is continually in motion, even when the user is not talking. The simulator sends the IM an non-speech message several times a second, giving the taxi's new position and heading. This information is passed to the DM, updating its state, and is essential for correct interpretation of commands like "Turn right at the next corner".

Considerations like these finally convinced us to move to a different strategy, in which offline regression testing more closely models the runtime behaviour of the application. At runtime, the system produces a time-stamped log of all input passed to the IM, including both speech and non-speech messages, in the sequence in which they were received. Each speech message is paired with a pointer to the recorded wavfile which produced it. Sets of such logs make up the test suite. Offline testing essentially re-runs the sequence of time-stamped records. Wavfiles are passed to a recognition server, which returns recognition results; time-stamps are used to set a notional internal clock, which replaces the real one for the purposes of performing temporal calculations. The test harness was quite easy to implement, and solves all the problems that arose from close adherence to a more speech recognition oriented test framework.

5 Using paraphrases at run-time

As mentioned in Section 3.2, paraphrase grammars can also be used at runtime, in order to provide a direct confirmation to the user showing how the system has interpreted what they have said. This is not a compelling design for every system; in a speech-only system, constant direct confirmation using paraphrases is in most cases unnatural and tedious. It is, however, a potentially valid strategy in a multi-modal system where it is possible to present a visual display of the paraphrase. In such a system, if paraphrases are regularly displayed to a user, there is, however, a good possibility of lexical and/or syntactic entrainment. Entrainment increases the likelihood that the user will produce the paraphrase language, which means that it would be valuable to be able to process that language through the system.

In the Regulus framework, this problem can be very straightforwardly addressed. Since the paraphrase grammar is a valid Regulus grammar, it can be compiled into a Nuance grammar, and hence into a second recognition package. At runtime, this package can be used in parallel with the main system recogniser. Because the paraphrase grammar is designed to directly relate surface language to dialogue moves, dialogue moves are generated directly, skipping the Input Manager processing. In particular, since the original point of the paraphrase grammar is to restate the user's content in a way that resolves and disambiguates underspecified material, there is no need for resolution processing. Figure 3 shows the dialogue system architecture with the additional paraphrase processing path.

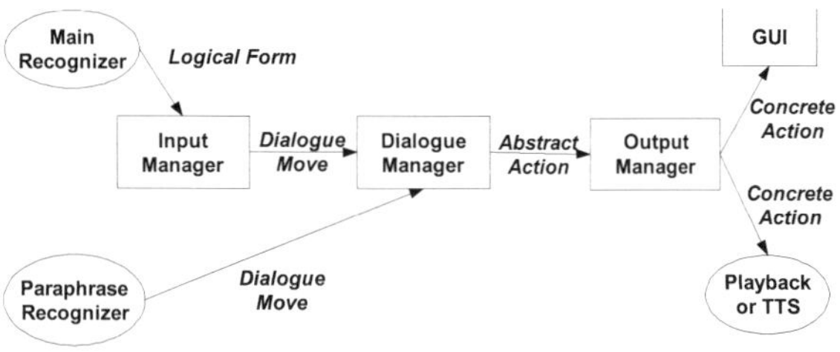

Figure 3: Regulus dialogue architecture with a processing path for paraphrases added. The paraphrase recognizer sends a dialogue move directly to the Dialogue Manager.

Although it may seem preferable to include the paraphrase coverage in the main recogniser coverage, we have found, somewhat to our surprise, that this is not nearly as straightforward as it first appears. The problem is that the two grammars are designed for very different tasks; the recognition grammar is intended to capture natural user language, while the paraphrase grammar's job is to produce unambiguous surface renderings of resolved semantic representations. Although we have endeavoured to make the paraphrase language as natural as possible, it is hard to avoid at least a few marginal constructions, which do not fit well into the structure of the normal recognition grammar; even if we did try to include them, the burden of keeping the two different grammars in synch would be considerable. From a software engineering point of view, it is far simpler just to maintain the two grammars separately, with each of them generating its own version of the recogniser.

We tested the paraphrase grammar recognizer for the Calendar application using paraphrases taken from a previous run log and recorded by the two authors. There were 249 recorded paraphrases total used. Because the Calendar paraphrase grammar had originally been designed with only visual display in mind, some augmentation of the paraphrase grammar was needed to cover the spoken versions of the paraphrases. There is often more than one possible spoken version corresponding to a written representation as was the case for this data. For example with a paraphrase such as "when are meetings on Sat Jan 3 2009", "Sat" could be pronounced "sat" or "Saturday", "3" could be "third" or "three", "Jan" could be produced as either "jan" or "January" and "2009" could be "two thousand nine" or "two thousand and nine". With the paraphrase component structured as a standard Regulus grammar, all that was needed was to add lexical items to cover the spoken variants. These additions were restricted to the recognition use of the paraphrase grammar and not used for generation. Word Error (WER) was 4.43% for the paraphrase grammar recognizer, Sentence Error (SER)was 34.53% and Semantic Error (SemER)was 17.9%. This SemER was calculated on untuned n-best. Clearly it is not possible to compare with the main recognizer on the same data, but for a rough comparison, we can look at numbers reported for the Calendar application in (Georgescul et al., 2008). That paper reports WER of 11.17% and SemER of 18.85% for the 1-best baseline. The SemER on the paraphrase grammar is 21.5% for 1-best. The paraphrase grammar recognizer has much better WER because it is so much more restricted than the main recognizer. However, the sentences covered by the paraphrase grammar are much longer than those covered in the main grammar, and this difference is reflected in the poorer performance by paraphrase grammar when measured in terms of SemER. The paraphrase language is long, very unnatural, yet we are able to produce a level of recognition performance that is quite usable.

Given the ability to recognize with the paraphrase grammar, a question which we hope to be able to investigate empirically is the effect that entrainment from exposure to the longer and less natural paraphrases actually has on user language, which initially tends to be biased towards short, natural-sounding utterances, with frequent use of ellipsis. This is a interesting topic for future research.

6 Conclusions

The dialogue move paraphrase mechanism provides a useful approach to streamlining regression testing without abandoning necessary detail. In non-trivial spoken dialogue systems, it is generally necessary to have a number of levels of representation. Our approach provides a middle ground between tracking each of these levels in the test suites, creating a excessive maintenance burden, and keeping only top level inputs and outputs, which is too coarse-grained to catch many errors. The Regulus framework provides the opportunity to implement this mechanism as a Regulus grammar, which makes the compilation into recognisers, parsers and generators available. While generation with the paraphrase grammar supports the described improvement in regression testing methodology, compiling the paraphrase grammar into a recogniser allows us to ensure that paraphrases used as confirmations can also be processed if directed at the dialogue system. The framework has been used with several fairly different kinds of applications, and appears to have a major impact on the overhead associated with maintenance of a useful regression testing regime.

References

J. Allen, D. Byron, M. Dzikovska, G. Ferguson, L. Galescu, and A. Stent. 2000. An architecture for a generic dialogue shell. *Natural Language Engineering, Special Issue on Best Practice in Spoken Language Dialogue Systems Engineering*, pages 1–16.

P. Bouillon, M. Rayner, B. Novellas, M. Starlander, M. Santaholma, Y. Nakao, and N. Chatzichrisafis. 2007. Une grammaire partagée multi-tâche pour le traitement de la parole: application aux langues romanes. *TAL.*

P. Bouillon, G. Flores, M. Georgescul, S. Halimi, B.A. Hockey, H. Isahara, K. Kanzaki, Y. Nakao, M. Rayner, M. Santaholma, M. Starlander, and N. Tsourakis. 2008. Many-to-many multilingual medical speech translation on a PDA. In *Proceedings of The Eighth Conference of the Association for Machine Translation in the Americas*, Waikiki, Hawaii.

Milica Gasić, Simon Keizer, Francois Mairesse, Jost Schatzmann, Blaise Thomson, Kai Yu, and Steve Young. 2008. Training and evaluation of the his pomdp dialogue system in noise. In *Proceedings of the 9th SIGDIAL Workshop on Discourse and Dialogue.*

Maria Georgescul, Manny Rayner, Pierrette Bouillon, and Nikos Tsourakis. 2008. Discriminative learning using linguistic features to rescore n-best speech hypotheses. In *The IEEE Workshop on Spoken Language Technology*, Goa, India.

S. Larsson and D. Traum. 2000. Information state and dialogue management in the TRINDI dialogue move engine toolkit. *Natural Language Engineering, Special Issue on Best Practice in Spoken Language Dialogue Systems Engineering*, pages 323–340.

M. Rayner, B.A. Hockey, J.M. Renders, N. Chatzichrisafis, and K. Farrell. 2005. A voice enabled procedure browser for the international space station. In *Proceedings of the 43rd Annual Meeting of the Association for Computational Linguistics (interactive poster and demo track)*, Ann Arbor, MI.

M. Rayner, B.A. Hockey, and P. Bouillon. 2006. *Putting Linguistics into Speech Recognition: The Regulus Grammar Compiler.* CSLI Press, Chicago.

M. Rayner. 1988. Applying explanation-based generalization to natural-language processing. In *Proceedings of the International Conference on Fifth Generation Computer Systems*, pages 1267–1274, Tokyo, Japan.

N. Roy, J Pineau, and S. Thrun. 2000. Spoken dialogue management using probabilistic reasoning. In *Proceedings of ACL*, Hong Kong.

N. Tsourakis, M. Georghescul, P. Bouillon, and M. Rayner. 2008. Building mobile spoken dialogue applications using regulus. In *Proceedings of LREC 2008*, Marrakesh, Morocco.

T. van Harmelen and A. Bundy. 1988. Explanation-based generalization = partial evaluation (research note). *Artificial Intelligence*, 36:401–412.

JD Williams and SJ Young. 2007. Partially observable markov decision processes for spoken dialog systems. *Computer Speech and Language.*

B. Zhang, Q Cai, J. Mao, E. Chang, and B Guo. 2001. Spoken dialogue management as planning and acting under uncertainty. In *Proceedings of Eurospeech*, Aalborg, Denmark.

Integrated NLP Evaluation System for Pluggable Evaluation Metrics with Extensive Interoperable Toolkit

Yoshinobu Kano[1] **Luke McCrohon**[1] **Sophia Ananiadou**[2] **Jun'ichi Tsujii**[1,2]

[1] Department of Computer Science, University of Tokyo
Hongo 7-3-1, Bunkyo-ku, Tokyo 113-0033 Tokyo

[2]School of Computer Science, University of Manchester and National Centre for Text Mining, 131 Princess St, M1 7DN, UK

[kano,tsujii]@is.s.u-tokyo.ac.jp
luke.mccrohon@gmail.com
sophia.ananiadou@manchester.ac.uk

Abstract

To understand the key characteristics of NLP tools, evaluation and comparison against different tools is important. And as NLP applications tend to consist of multiple semi-independent sub-components, it is not always enough to just evaluate complete systems, a fine grained evaluation of underlying components is also often worthwhile. Standardization of NLP components and resources is not only significant for reusability, but also in that it allows the comparison of individual components in terms of reliability and robustness in a wider range of target domains. But as many evaluation metrics exist in even a single domain, any system seeking to aid inter-domain evaluation needs not just predefined metrics, but must also support pluggable user-defined metrics. Such a system would of course need to be based on an open standard to allow a large number of components to be compared, and would ideally include visualization of the differences between components. We have developed a pluggable evaluation system based on the UIMA framework, which provides visualization useful in error analysis. It is a single integrated system which includes a large ready-to-use, fully interoperable library of NLP tools.

1 Introduction

When building NLP applications, the same subtasks tend to appear frequently while constructing different systems. Due to this, the reusability of tools designed for such subtasks is a common design consideration; fine grained interoperability between sub components, not just between complete systems.

In addition to the benefits of reusability, interoperability is also important in evaluation of components. Evaluations are normally done by comparing two sets of data, a gold standard data and test data showing the components performance. Naturally this comparison requires the two data sets to be in the same data format with the same semantics. Comparing of "Apples to Apples" provides another reason why standardization of NLP tools is beneficial. Another advantage of standardization is that the number of gold standard data sets that can be compared against is also increased, allowing tools to be tested in a wider range of domains.

The ideal is that all components are standardized to conform to an open, widely used interoperability framework. One possible such framework is UIMA; Unstructured Information Management Architecture (Ferrucci et al., 2004), which is an open project of OASIS and Apache. We have been developing U-Compare (Kano et al., 2009)[1], an integrated testing an evaluation platform based on this framework.

[1] Features described in this paper are integrated as U-Compare system, publicly available from: http://u-compare.org/

Proceedings of the NAACL HLT Workshop on Software Engineering, Testing, and Quality Assurance for Natural Language Processing, pages 22–30,
Boulder, Colorado, June 2009.

Although U-Compare already provided a wide range of tools and NLP resources, its inbuilt evaluation mechanisms were hard coded into the system and were not customizable by end users. Furthermore the evaluation metrics used were based only on simple strict matchings which severely limited its domains of application. We have extended the evaluation mechanism to allow users to define their own metrics which can be integrated into the range of existing evaluation tools.

The U-Compare library of interoperable tools has also been extended; especially with regard to resources related to biomedical named entity extraction. U-Compare is currently providing the world largest library of type system compatible UIMA components.

In section 2 of this paper we first look at the underlying technologies, UIMA and U-Compare. Then we describe the new pluggable evaluation mechanism in section 3 and our interoperable toolkit with our type system in section 4 and 5.

2 Background

2.1 UIMA

UIMA is an open framework specified by OASIS[2]. Apache UIMA provides a reference implementation as an open source project, with both a pure java API and a C++ development kit . UIMA itself is intended to be purely a framework, i.e. it does not intend to provide specific tools or type system definitions. Users should develop such resources themselves. In the following subsections, we briefly describe the basic concepts of UIMA, and define keywords used to explain our system in later sections.

2.1.1 CAS and Type System

The UIMA framework uses the "stand-off annotation" style (Ferrucci et al., 2006). The underling raw text of a document is generally kept unchanged during analysis, and the results of processing the text are added as new stand-off annotations with references to their positions in the raw text. A *Common Analysis Structure* (*CAS*) holds a set of such annotations. Each of which is of a given *type* as defined in a specified hierarchical *type system*. Annotation[3] types may define features, which are themselves typed. Apache UIMA provides definitions of a range of built in primitive types, but a more complete type system should be specified by developers. The top level Apache UIMA type is referred to as TOP, other primitive types include. int, String, Annotation and FSArray (an array of any annotations).

2.1.2 Component and Capability

UIMA components receive and update CAS one at a time. Each UIMA component has a *capability* property, which describes what *types* of annotations it takes as input and what *types* of annotations it may produce as output.

UIMA components can be deployed either locally, or remotely as SOAP web services. Remotely deployed web service components and locally deployed components can be freely combined in UIMA workflows.

2.1.3 Aggregate Component and Flow Controller

UIMA components can be either *primitive* or *aggregate*. Aggregate components include other components as subcomponents. Subcomponents may themselves be aggregate. In the case where an aggregate has multiple subcomponents these are by default processed in linear order. This ordering can be customized by implementing a custom *flow controller*.

2.2 U-Compare

U-Compare is a joint project of the University of Tokyo, the Center for Computational Pharmacology at the University of Colorado School of Medicine, and the UK National Centre for Text Mining.

U-Compare provides an integrated platform for users to construct, edit and compare workflows compatible with any UIMA component. It also provides a large, ready-to-use toolkit of interoperable NLP components for use with any UIMA based system. This toolkit is currently the world largest repository of type system compatible components. These all implement the U-Compare type system described in section 3.

[2] http://www.oasis-open.org/committees/uima/

[3] In the UIMA framework, Annotation is a base *type* which has *begin* and *end* offset values. In this paper we call any objects (any subtype of TOP) as *annotations*.

2.2.1 Related Works

There also exist several other public UIMA component repositories: CMU UIMA component repository, BioNLP UIMA repository (Baumgartner et al., 2008), JCoRe (Hahn et al., 2008), Tsujii Lab Component Repository at the University of Tokyo (Kano et al., 2008a), etc. Each group uses their own type system, and so components provided by each group are incompatible. Unlike U-Compare these repositories are basically only collections of UIMA components, U-Compare goes further by providing a fully integrated set of UIMA tools and utilities.

2.2.2 Integrated Platform

U-Compare provides a variety of features as part of an integrated platform. The system can be launched with a single click in a web browser; all required libraries are downloaded and updated automatically in background.

The Workflow Manager GUI helps users to create workflows in an easy drag-and-drop fashion. Similarly, import/export of workflows, running of workflows and saving results can all be handled via a graphical interface.

U-Compare special parallel aggregate components allow combinations of specified components to be automatically combined and compared based on their I/O capabilities (Kano et al., 2008b). When workflows are run, U-Compare shows statistics and visualizations of results appropriate to the type of workflow. For example when workflows including parallel aggregate components are run comparison statistics between all possible parallel component combinations are given.

3 Integrated System for Pluggable Evaluation Metrics

While U-Compare already has a mechanism to automatically create possible combinations of components for comparison from a specified workflow, the comparison (evaluation) metric itself was hard coded into the system. Only comparison based on simple strict matching was possible.

However, many different evaluation metrics exist, even for the same type of annotations. For example, named entity recognition results are often evaluated based on several different annotation intersection criteria: exact match, left/right only match, overlap, etc. Evaluation metrics for nested components can be even more complex (e.g. biomedical relations, deep syntactic structures). Sometimes new metrics are also required for specific tasks. Thus, a mechanism for pluggable evaluation metrics in a standardized way is seen as desirable.

3.1 Pluggable Evaluation Component

Our design goal for the evaluation systems is to do as much of the required work as possible and to provide utilities to reduce developer's labor. We also want our design to be generic and fix within existing UIMA standards.

The essential process of evaluation can be generalized and decomposed as follows:

(a) prepare a pair of annotation sets which will be used for comparison,

(b) select annotations which should be included in the final evaluation step,

(c) compare selected annotations against each other and mark matched pairs.

For example, in the case of the Penn Treebank style syntactic bracket matching, these steps correspond to (a) prepare two sets of constituents and tokens, (b) select only the constituents (removing null elements if required), (c) compare constituents between the sets and return any matches.

In our new design, step (a) is performed by the system, (b) and (c) are performed by an evaluation component. The evaluation component is just a normal UIMA component, pluggable based on the UIMA standard. This component is run on a CAS which was constructed by the system during step (a). This CAS includes an instance of ComparisonSet type and its features GoldAnnotationGroup and TestAnnotationGroup. Corresponding to step (b), based on this input the comparison component should make a selection of annotations and store them as FSArray for both GoldAnnotations and TestAnnotations. Finally for step (c), the component should perform a matching and store the results as MatchedPair instances in the MatchedAnnotations feature of the ComparisonSet.

Precision, recall, and F1 scores are calculated by U-Compare based on the outputted ComparisonSet. These calculation can be overridden and customized if the developer so desires.

Implementation of the `compare()` method of the evaluation component is recommended. It is used by the system when showing instance based evaluations of what feature values are used in matching, which features are matched, and which are not.

3.2 Combinatorial Evaluation and Error Analysis

By default, evaluation statistics are calculated by simply counting the numbers of gold, test, matched annotations in the returned ComparisonSet instance. Then precision, recall, and F1 scores for each CAS and for the complete set of CASes are calculated. Users can specify which evaluation metrics are used for each *type* of annotations based on the input specifications they set for supplied evaluation components.

Normally, precision, recall, and F1 scores are the only evaluation statistics used in the NLP community. It is often the case in many research reports that a new tool A performs better than another tool B, increasing the F1 score by 1%. In such cases it is important to analysis what proportion of annotations are shared between A, B, and the gold standard. Is A a strict 1% increase over B? Or does it cover 2% of instances B doesn't but miss a different 1%? Our system provides these statistics as well.

Further, our standardized evaluation system makes more advanced evaluation available. Since the evaluation metrics themselves are more or less arbitrary, we should carefully observe the results of evaluations. When two or more metrics are available for the same type of annotations, we can compare the results of each to analyze and validate the individual evaluations.

An immediate application of such comparison would be in a voting system, which takes the results of several tools as input and selects common overlapping annotations as output.

U-Compare also provides visualizations of evaluation results allowing instance-based error analysis.

4 U-Compare Type System

U-Compare currently provides the world largest set of type system compatible UIMA components. We will describe some of these in section 5. In creating compatible components in UIMA a key task is their *type system* definitions.

The U-Compare type system is designed in a hierarchical fashion with distinct types to achieve a high level of interoperability. It is intended to be a shared type system capable of mapping types originally defined as part of independent type systems (Kano et al., 2008c). In this section we describe the U-Compare type system in detail.

4.1 Basic Types

While most of the U-Compare types are inheriting a UIMA built-in type, Annotation (Figure 1), there are also types directly extending the TOP type; let us call these types as metadata types.

AnnotationMetadata holds a confidence value, which is common to all of the U-Compare annotation types as a feature of BaseAnnotation type. BaseAnnotation extends DiscontinuousAnnotation, in which fragmental annotations can be stored as a FSArray of Annotations, if any.

ExternalReference is another common metadata type where namespace and ID are stored, referring to an external ontology entity outside UIMA/U-Compare. Because it is not realistic to represent everything like such a detailed ontology hierarchy in a UIMA type system, this metadata is used to recover original information, which are not expressed as UIMA types. ReferenceAnnotation is another base annotation type, which holds an instance of this ExternalReference.

UniqueLabel is a special top level type for explicitly defined finite label sets, e.g. the Penn Treebank tagset. Each label in such a tagset is mapped to a single type where UniqueLabel as its

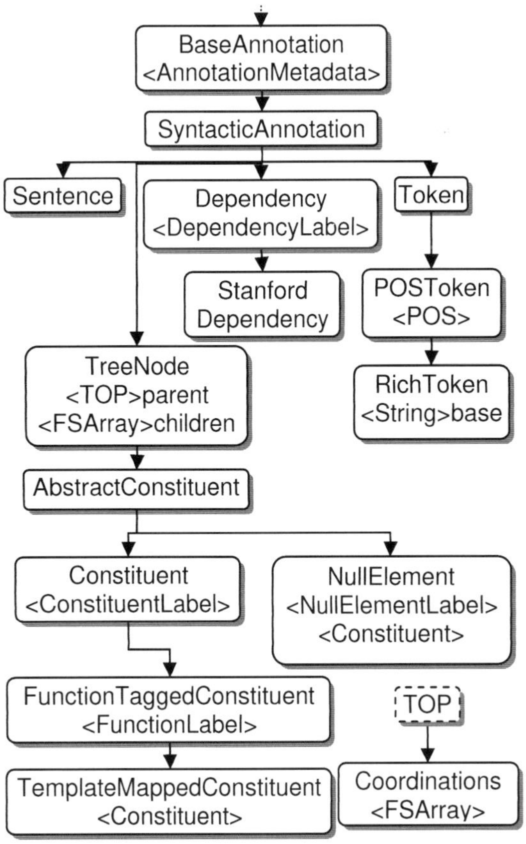

Figure 2. Syntactic Types in U-Compare.

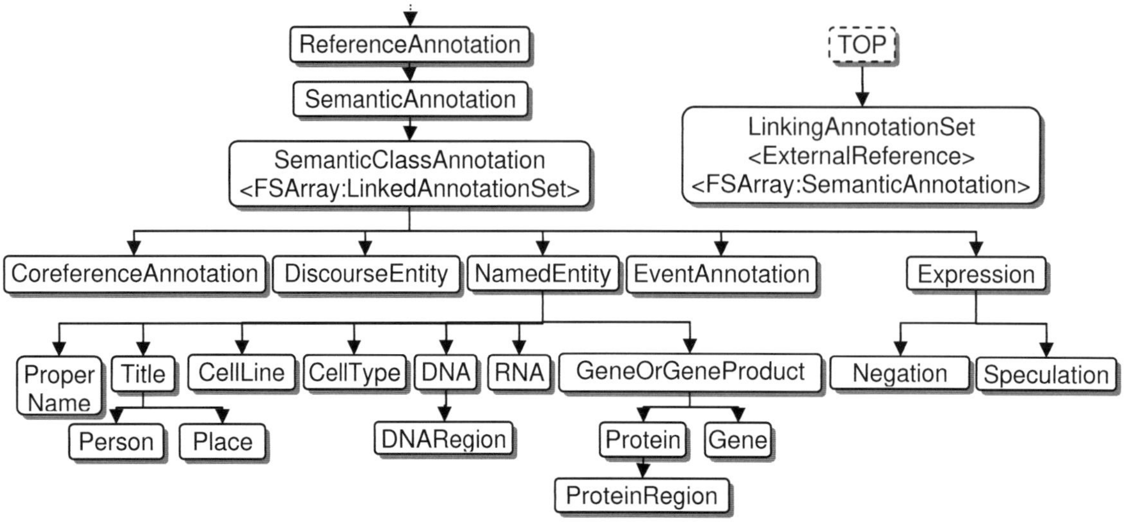

Figure 3. Semantic types in the U-Compare type system.

ancestor, putting middle level types if possible (e.g. Noun type for the Penn Treebank POS tag-set). These types are omitted in the figure.

4.2 Syntactic Types

SyntacticAnnotation is the base type of all syntactic types (Figure 2). POSToken holds a POS label, RichToken additionally holds a base form. Dependency is used by dependency parsers, while TreeNode is for syntactic tree nodes. Constituent, NullElement, FunctionTaggedConstituent, TemplateMappedConstituent are designed to fully represent all of the Penn Treebank style annotations. Coordination is a set of references to coordinating nodes (currently used by the Genia Treebank). We are planning on extending the set of syntactic types to cover the outputs of several deep parsers.

4.3 Semantic Types

SemanticAnnotation is the base type for semantic annotations; it extends ReferenceAnnotation by holding the original reference.

SemanticClassAnnotation is a rather complex type designed to be somewhat general. In many cases, semantic annotations may reference other semantic annotations, e.g. references between biological events. Such references are often labeled with their roles which we express with the ExternalReference type. Such labeled references are expressed by LinkingAnnotationSet. As a role may refer to more than one annotation, LinkingAnnotationSet has an FSArray of SemanticAnnotation as a feature.

There are several biomedical types included in Figure 3, e.g. DNA, RNA, Protein, Gene, CellLine, CellType, etc. It is however difficult to decide which ontological entities should be included in such a type system. One reason for this is that such concepts are not always distinct; different ontologies may give overlapping definitions of these concepts. Further, the number of possible substance level entities is infinite; causing difficult in their expression as individual types. The current set of biomedical types in the U-Compare type system includes types which are frequently used for evaluation in the BioNLP research.

4.4 Document Types

DocumentAnnotation is the base type for document related annotations (Figure 4). It extends

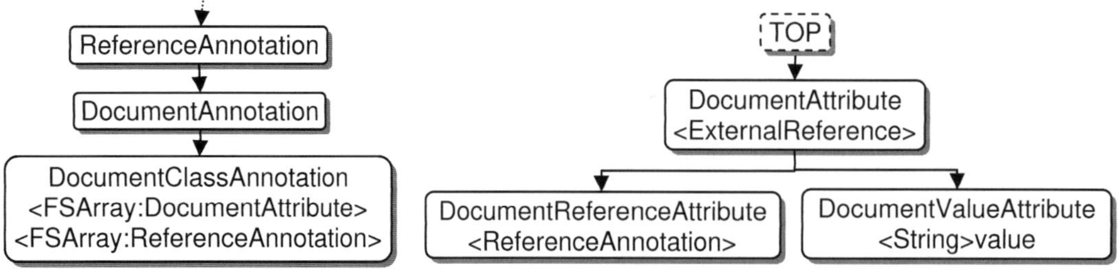

Figure 4. Document types in the U-Compare type system.

ReferenceAnnotation to reference the full external type in the same way as SemanticAnnotation.

DocumentClassAnnotation together with DocumentAttribute are intended to express XML style data. XML tags may have fields storing their values, and/or idref fields refering to other tags. DocumentValueAttiributerepresents simple value field, while DocumentReferenceAttribute represents idref type fields. A DocumentClassAnnotation corresponds to the tag itself.

Although these types can represent most document structures, we still plan to add several specific types such as Paragraph, Title, etc.

5 Interoperable Components and Utilities

In this section, we describe our extensive toolkit of interoperable components and the set of utilities integrated into the U-Compare system. All of the components in our toolkit are compatible with the U-Compare type system described in the previous section.

5.1 Corpus Reader Components

In the UIMA framework, a component which generates CASes is called a *Collection Reader*. We have developed several collection readers which read annotated corpora and generates annotations using the U-Compare type system.

Because our primary target domain was biomedical field, there are corpus readers for the biomedical corpora; Aimed corpus (Bunescu et al., 2006) reader and BioNLP '09 shared task format reader generate event annotations like protein-protein interaction annotations; Readers for BIO/IOB format, Bio1 corpus (Tateisi et al., 2000), BioCreative (Hirschman et al., 2004) task 1a format, BioIE corpus (Bies et al., 2005), NLPBA shared task dataset (Kim et al., 2004), Texas Corpus (Bunescu et al., 2005), Yapex Corpus (Kristofer Franzen et al., 2002), generate biomedical named entities, and Genia Treebank corpus (Tateisi et al., 2005) reader generates Penn Treebank (Marcus et al., 1993) style bracketing and part-of-speech annotations. Format readers require users to prepare annotated data, while others include corpora themselves, automatically downloaded as an archive on users' demand.

In addition, there is File System Collection Reader from Apache UIMA which reads files as plain text. We have developed an online interactive text reader, named Input Text Reader.

```
187
The document length in bytes is
output in the first line (end with
new line),
then the raw text follows as is
(attaching a new line in the end),
finally annotations follow line by
line.
0 187 Document id="u1"
0 3 POSToken id="u2" pos="DT"
....
```

Figure 5. An example of the U-Compare simple I/O format.

5.2 Analysis Engine Components

There are many tools covering from basic syntactic annotations to the biomedical annotations. Some of the tools are running as web services, but users can freely mix local services and web services.

For syntactic annotations: sentence detectors from GENIA, LingPipe, NaCTeM, OpenNLP and Apache UIMA; tokenizers from GENIA tagger (Tsuruoka et al., 2005), OpenNLP, Apache UIMA and Penn Bio Tokenizer; POS taggers from GENIA tagger, LingPipe, OpenNLP and Stepp Tagger; parsers from OpenNLP (CFG), Stanford Parser (dependency) (de Marneffe et al., 2006), Enju (HPSG) (Miyao et al., 2008).

For semantic annotations: ABNER (Settles, 2005) for NLPBA/BioCreative trained models, GENIA Tagger, NeMine, MedT-NER, LingPipe and OpenNLP NER, for named entity recognitions. Akane++ (Sætre et al., 2007) for protein-protein interaction detections.

5.3 Components for Developers

Although Apache UIMA provides APIs in both Java and C++ to help users develop UIMA components, a level of understanding of the UIMA framework is still required. Conversion of existing tools to the UIMA framework can also be difficult, particularly when they are written in other programming languages.

We have designed a simple I/O format to make it easy for developers who just want to provide a UIMA wrapper for existing tools.

Input of this format consists of two parts: raw text and annotations The first line of the raw text section is an integer of byte count of the length of the text. The raw text then follows with a newline character appended at the end. Annotations are then included; one annotation per line, sometimes referring another annotation by assigned ids (Figure 5). A line consists of begin position,

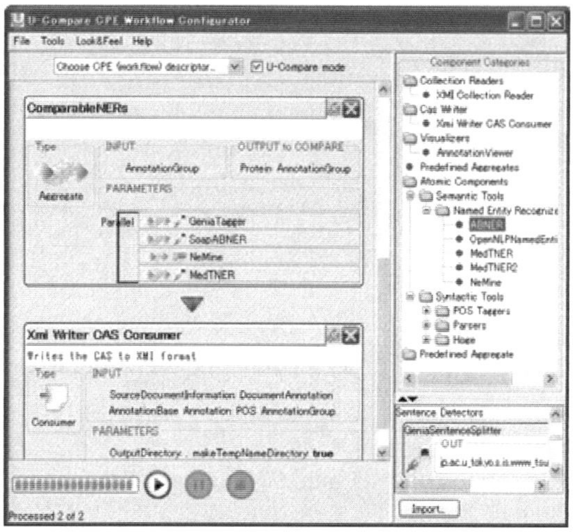

Figure 6. A screenshot of Workflow Manager GUI and Component Library.

end position, type name, unique id, and feature values if any. Double newlines indicates an end of a CAS.

Output of the component is lines of annotations if any created by the component.

U-Compare provides a wrapper component which uses this I/O format, communicating with wrapped tools via standard I/O streams.

5.4 Type System Converters

As U-Compare is a joint project, the U-Compare toolkit includes UIMA components originally developed using several different type systems. In order to integrate these components into the U-Compare type system, we have developed type system converter components for each external type system.

The CCP team at the University of Colorado made a converter between their CCP type system and our type system. We also developed converters for OpenNLP components and Apache UIMA components. These converters remove any original annotations not compatible with the U-Compare type system. This prevents duplicated converters from translating external annotation multiple times in the same workflow.

We are providing such non U-Compare components by aggregating with type system converters, so users do not need to aware of the type system conversions.

5.5 Utility Tools

We have developed and integrated several utility tools, especially GUI tools for usability and error analysis.

Figure 6 is showing our workflow manager GUI, which provides functions to create a user workflow by an easy drag-and-drop way. By clicking "Run Workflow" button in that manager window, statistics will be shown (Figure 8).

There are also a couple of annotation visualization tools. Figure 7 is showing a viewer for tree structures and HPSG feature structures. Figure 9 is showing a general annotation viewer, when annotations have complex inter-dependencies.

6 Summary and Future Directions

We have designed and developed a pluggable evaluation system based on the UIMA framework. This evaluation system is integrated with the U-Compare combinatorial comparison mechanism which makes evaluation of many factors available automatically.

Since the system behavior is dependent on the type system used, we have carefully designed the U-Compare type system to cover a broad range of concepts used in NLP applications. Based directly on this type system, or using type system converters, we have developed a large toolkit of type system compatible interoperable UIMA component. All of these features are integrated into U-Compare.

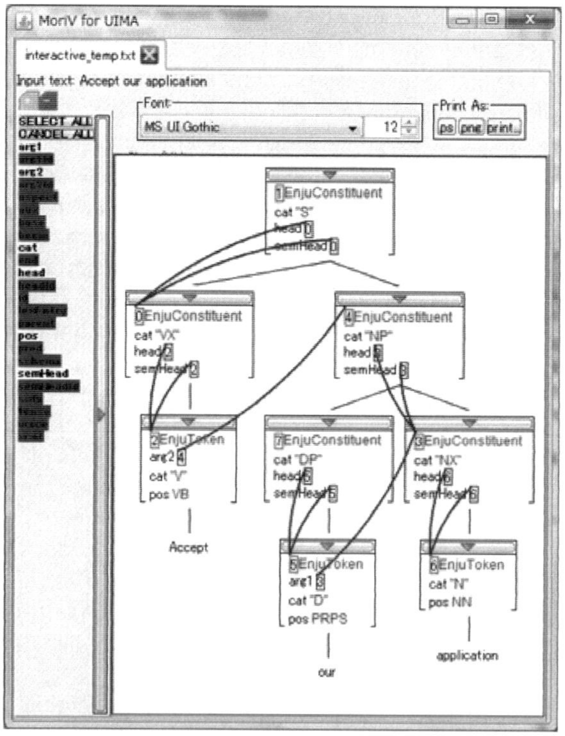

Figure 7. A screenshot of HPSG feature structure viewer, showing a skeleton CFG tree, feature values and head/semhead links.

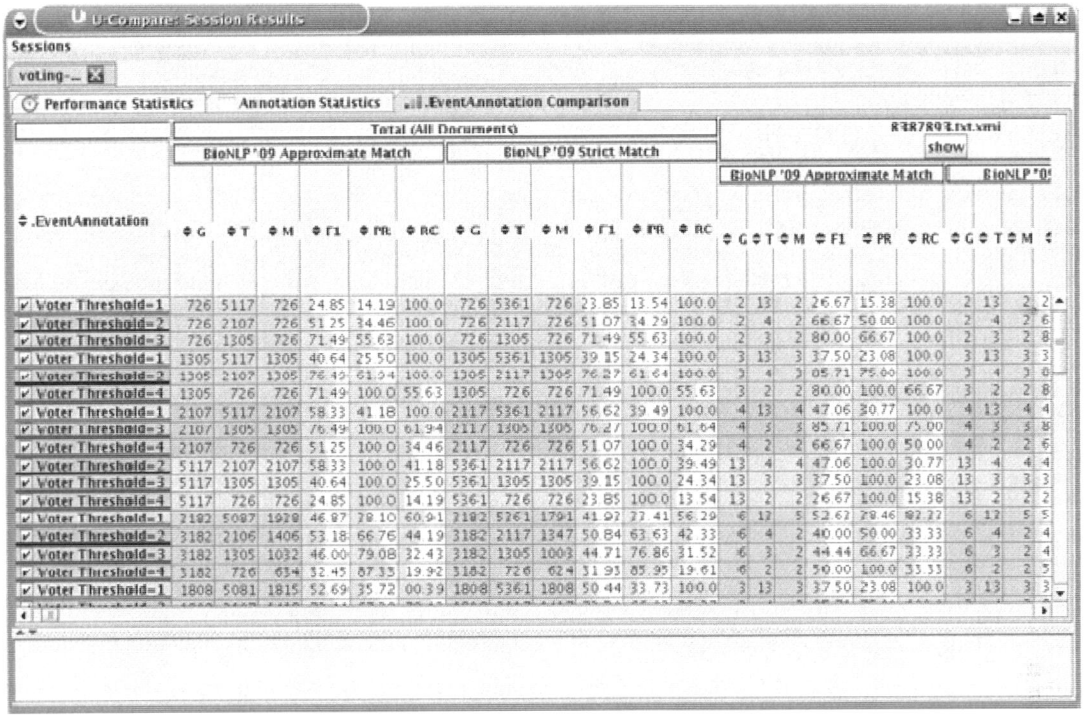

Figure 8. A screenshot of a comparison statistics showing number of instances (gold, test, and matched), F1, precision, and recall scores of two evaluation metrics on the same data.

In future we are planning to increase the number of components available, e.g. more syntactic parsers, corpus readers, and resources for languages other than English. This will also required enhancements to the existing type system to support additional components. Finally we also hope to add integration with machine learning tools in the near future.

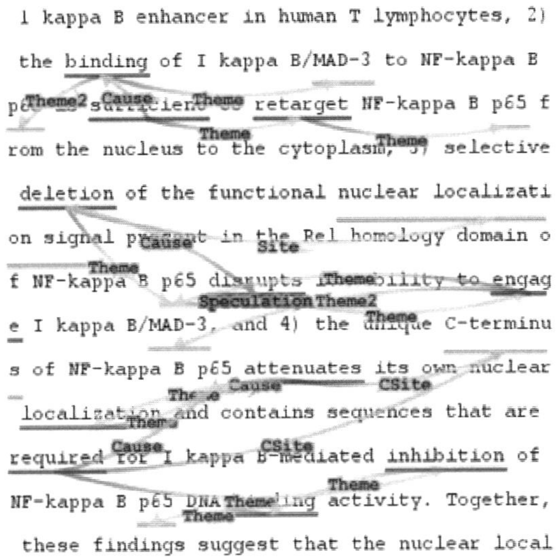

Figure 9. A screenshot of a visualization of complex annotations.

Acknowledgments

We wish to thank Dr. Lawrence Hunter's text mining group at Center for Computational Pharmacology, University of Colorado School of Medicine, for helping build the type system and for making their tools available for this research. This work was partially supported by Grant-in-Aid for Specially Promoted Research (MEXT, Japan). The National Centre for Text Mining is funded by JISC.

References

W. A. Baumgartner, Jr., K. B. Cohen, and L. Hunter. 2008. *An open-source framework for large-scale, flexible evaluation of biomedical text mining systems.* J Biomed Discov Collab, 3(1), 1.

Ann Bies, Seth Kulick, and Mark Mandel. 2005. *Parallel entity and treebank annotation.* In Proceedings of the the Workshop on Frontiers in Corpus Annotations II: Pie in the Sky, ACL, Ann Arbor, Michigan, USA.

Razvan Bunescu, Ruifang Ge, Rohit J. Kate, Edward M. Marcotte, Raymond J. Mooney, Arun Kumar Ramani, et al. 2005. *Comparative experiments on learning information extractors for proteins and their interactions.* Artificial Intelligence in Medicine, 33(2), 139-155.

Razvan Bunescu, and Raymond Mooney. 2006. *Subsequence Kernels for Relation Extraction.* In Y. Weiss, B. Scholkopf and J. Platt (Eds.), *Advances in Neural Information Processing Systems 18* (171--178). Cambridge, MA: MIT Press.

Marie-Catherine de Marneffe, Bill MacCartney, and Christopher D. Manning. 2006. *Generating typed dependency parses from phrase structure parses.* In Proceedings of the the 5th International Conference on Language Resources and Evaluation (LREC 2006).

David Ferrucci, and Adam Lally. 2004. *Building an example application with the Unstructured Information Management Architecture.* Ibm Systems Journal, 43(3), 455-475.

David Ferrucci, Adam Lally, Daniel Gruhl, and Edward Epstein. 2006. *Towards an Interoperability Standard for Text and Multi-Modal Analytics.*

U. Hahn, E. Buyko, R. Landefeld, M. Mühlhausen, M. Poprat, K. Tomanek, et al. 2008, May. *An Overview of JCoRe, the JULIE Lab UIMA Component Repository.* In Proceedings of the LREC'08 Workshop, Towards Enhanced Interoperability for Large HLT Systems: UIMA for NLP, Marrakech, Morocco.

Lynette Hirschman, Alexander Yeh, Christian Blaschke, and Antonio Valencia. 2004. *Overview of BioCreAtIvE: critical assessment of information extraction for biology.* BMC Bionformatics, 6(Suppl 1:S1).

Yoshinobu Kano, William A Baumgartner, Luke McCrohon, Sophia Ananiadou, Kevin B Cohen, Lawrence Hunter, et al. 2009. *U-Compare: share and compare text mining tools with UIMA.* Bioinformatics, accepted.

Yoshinobu Kano, Ngan Nguyen, Rune Sætre, Keiichiro Fukamachi, Kazuhiro Yoshida, Yusuke Miyao, et al. 2008c, January. *Sharable type system design for tool inter-operability and combinatorial comparison.* In Proceedings of the the First International Conference on Global Interoperability for Language Resources (ICGL), Hong Kong.

Yoshinobu Kano, Ngan Nguyen, Rune Sætre, Kazuhiro Yoshida, Keiichiro Fukamachi, Yusuke Miyao, et al. 2008b, January. *Towards Data And Goal Oriented Analysis: Tool Inter-Operability And Combinatorial Comparison.* In Proceedings of the 3rd International Joint Conference on Natural Language Processing (IJCNLP), Hyderabad, India.

Yoshinobu Kano, Ngan Nguyen, Rune Sætre, Kazuhiro Yoshida, Yusuke Miyao, Yoshimasa Tsuruoka, et al. 2008a, January. *Filling the gaps between tools and users: a tool comparator, using protein-protein interaction as an example.* In Proceedings of the Pacific Symposium on Biocomputing (PSB), Hawaii, USA.

Jin-Dong Kim, Tomoko Ohta, Yoshimasa Tsuruoka, Yuka Tateisi, and Nigel Collier. 2004. *Introduction to the Bio-Entity Recognition Task at JNLPBA.* In Proceedings of the International Workshop on Natural Language Processing in Biomedicine and its Applications (JNLPBA-04), Geneva, Switzerland.

Kristofer Franzen, Gunnar Eriksson, Fredrik Olsson, Lars Asker, Per Liden, and Joakim Coster. 2002. *Protein names and how to find them.* International Journal of Medical Informatics, 67(1-3), 49-61.

Mitchell P. Marcus, Mary Ann Marcinkiewicz, and Beatrice Santorini. 1993. *Building a large annotated corpus of English: the penn treebank.* Computational Linguistics, 19(2), 313-330.

Yusuke Miyao, and Jun'ichi Tsujii. 2008. *Feature Forest Models for Probabilistic HPSG Parsing.* Computational Linguistics, 34(1), 35-80.

Rune Sætre, Kazuhiro Yoshida, Akane Yakushiji, Yusuke Miyao, Yuichiro Matsubayashi, and Tomoko Ohta. 2007, April. *AKANE System: Protein-Protein Interaction Pairs in BioCreAtIvE2 Challenge, PPI-IPS subtask.* In Proceedings of the Second BioCreative Challenge Evaluation Workshop.

Burr Settles. 2005. *ABNER: an open source tool for automatically tagging genes, proteins and other entity names in text.* Bioinformatics, 21(14), 3191-3192.

Yuka Tateisi, Tomoko Ohta, Nigel Collier, Chikashi Nobata, and Jun'ichi Tsujii. 2000, August. *Building an Annotated Corpus from Biology Research Papers.* In Proceedings of the COLING 2000 Workshop on Semantic Annotation and Intelligent Content, Luxembourg.

Yuka Tateisi, Akane Yakushiji, Tomoko Ohta, and Jun'ichi Tsujii. 2005, October. *Syntax Annotation for the GENIA Corpus.* In Proceedings of the the Second International Joint Conference on Natural Language Processing (IJCNLP '05), Companion volume, Jeju Island, Korea.

Yoshimasa Tsuruoka, Yuka Tateishi, Jin Dong Kim, Tomoko Ohta, J. McNaught, Sophia Ananiadou, et al. 2005. *Developing a robust part-of-speech tagger for biomedical text.* In *Advances in Informatics, Proceedings* (Vol. 3746, 382-392). Berlin: Springer-Verlag Berlin.

Tightly Packed Tries: How to Fit Large Models into Memory, and Make them Load Fast, Too

Ulrich Germann
University of Toronto and
National Research Council Canada
germann@cs.toronto.edu

Eric Joanis
National Research Council Canada
Eric.Joanis@cnrc-nrc.gc.ca

Samuel Larkin
National Research Council Canada
Samuel.Larkin@cnrc-nrc.gc.ca

Abstract

We present *Tightly Packed Tries* (TPTs), a compact implementation of read-only, compressed trie structures with fast on-demand paging and short load times.

We demonstrate the benefits of TPTs for storing n-gram back-off language models and phrase tables for statistical machine translation. Encoded as TPTs, these databases require less space than flat text file representations of the same data compressed with the *gzip* utility. At the same time, they can be mapped into memory quickly and be searched directly in time linear in the length of the key, without the need to decompress the entire file. The overhead for local decompression during search is marginal.

1 Introduction

The amount of data available for data-driven Natural Language Processing (NLP) continues to grow. For some languages, language models (LM) are now being trained on many billions of words, and parallel corpora available for building statistical machine translation (SMT) systems can run into tens of millions of sentence pairs. This wealth of data allows the construction of bigger, more comprehensive models, often without changes to the fundamental model design, for example by simply increasing the n-gram size in language modeling or the phrase length in phrase tables for SMT.

The large sizes of the resulting models pose an engineering challenge. They are often too large to fit entirely in main memory. What is the best way to organize these models so that we can swap information in and out of memory as needed, and as quickly as possible?

This paper presents *Tightly Packed Tries* (TPTs), a compact and fast-loading implementation of read-only trie structures for NLP databases that store information associated with token sequences, such as language models, n-gram count databases, and phrase tables for SMT.

In the following section, we first recapitulate some basic data structures and encoding techniques that are the foundations of TPTs. We then lay out the organization of TPTs. Section 3 discusses compression of node values (i.e., the information associated with each key). Related work is discussed in Section 4. In Section 5, we report empirical results from run-time tests of TPTs in comparison to other implementations. Section 6 concludes the paper.

2 Fundamental data structures and encoding techniques

2.1 Tries

Tries (Fredkin, 1960), also known as *prefix trees*, are a well-established data structure for compactly storing sets of strings that have common prefixes. Each string is represented by a single node in a tree structure with labeled arcs so that the sequence of arc labels from the root node to the respective node "spells out" the token sequence in question. If we augment the trie nodes with additional information, tries can be used as indexing structures for databases that rely on token sequences as search keys. For the remainder of this paper, we will refer to such additional

Proceedings of the NAACL HLT Workshop on Software Engineering, Testing, and Quality Assurance for Natural Language Processing, pages 31–39,
Boulder, Colorado, June 2009.

total count	20
a	13
aa	10
ab	3
b	7

(a) Count table

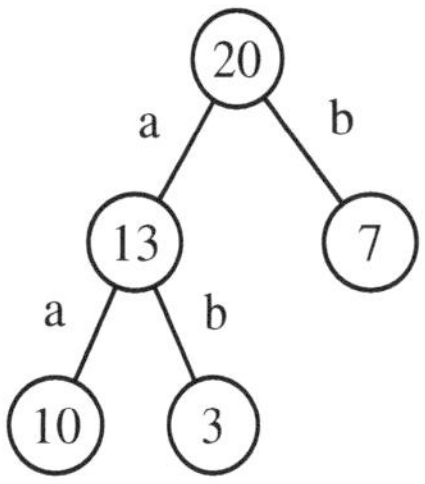

(b) Trie representation

field	32-bit	64-bit
index entry: token ID	4	4
index entry: pointer	4	8
start of index (pointer)	4	8
overhead of index structure node value	x	y
total (in bytes)	$12 + x$	$20 + y$

(c) Memory footprint per node in an implementation using memory pointers

0	13	*offset of root node*
1	10	*node value of* 'aa'
2	0	*size of index to child nodes of* 'aa' in bytes
3	3	*node value of* 'ab'
4	0	*size of index to child nodes of* 'ab' in bytes
5	13	*node value of* 'a'
6	4	*size of index to child nodes of 'a' in bytes*
7	a	*index key for* 'aa' *coming from* 'a'
8	4	*relative offset of node* 'aa' $(5 - 4 = 1)$
9	b	*index key for* 'ab' *coming from* 'a'
10	2	*relative offset of node* 'ab' $(5 - 2 = 3)$
11	7	*node value of* 'b'
12	0	*size of index to child nodes of* 'b' in bytes
13	20	*root node value*
14	4	*size of index to child nodes of root in bytes*
15	a	*index key for* 'a' *coming from root*
16	8	*relative offset of node* 'a' $(13 - 8 = 5)$
17	b	*index key for* 'b' *coming from root*
18	2	*relative offset of node* 'b' $(13 - 2 = 11)$

(d) Trie representation in a contiguous byte array. In practice, each field may vary in length.

Figure 1: A count table (a) stored in a trie structure (b) and the trie's sequential representation in a file (d). As the size of the count table increases, the trie-based storage becomes more efficient, provided that the keys have common prefixes. (c) shows the memory footprint per trie node when the trie is implemented as a mutable structure using direct memory pointers.

information as the *node value*. Figure 1b shows a count table (Figure 1a) represented as a trie.

Tries offer two main advantages over other indexing structures, e.g., binary search trees. First, they are more compact because overlapping prefixes are stored only once. And second, unless the set of keys is extremely small, lookup is faster than with binary search trees. While the latter need time logarithmic in the number of keys, trie-based search is linear in the length of the search key.

2.2 Representing tries in memory

Mutable trie implementations usually represent tries as collections of fixed-size records containing the node value and a pointer or reference to an indexing structure (henceforth: *index*) that maps from arc or token labels to the respective child nodes. Links to child nodes are represented by object references or C-style memory pointers. To simplify the discussion, we assume in the following that the code consistently uses pointers. Since integers are faster to compare and require less space to store than character strings, token labels are best represented as integer IDs. With typical vocabulary sizes ranging from hundreds of thousands to several million distinct items, 32-bit integers are the data type of choice to store token IDs.[1]

This type of implementation offers flexibility and fast lookup but has two major drawbacks. First, load times are significant (cf. Tables 1 and 3). Since each node is created individually, the entire trie must be traversed at load time. In addition, all the information contained in the database must be copied explicitly from the OS-level file cache into the current process's memory.

Second, these implementations waste memory, especially on 64-bit machines. Depending on the architecture, memory pointers require 4 or 8 byes of memory. In theory, a 64-bit pointer allows us to address 16 exabytes (16 million terabytes) of memory. In practice, 20 to 30 bits per 64-bit pointer will remain unused on most state-of-the-art computing equipment.

The use of 32-bit integers to represent token IDs also wastes memory. Even for large corpora, the size

[1] 16 bits have been used occasionally in the past (Clarkson and Rosenfeld, 1997; Whittaker and Raj, 2001) but limit the vocabulary ca. 64 K tokens.

of the token vocabulary is on the order of several million distinct items or below. The Google 1T web n-gram database (Brants and Franz, 2006), for example, has a vocabulary of only ca. 13 million distinct items, which can be represented in 24 bits, letting 8 bits go to waste if IDs are represented as 32-bit integers.

An alternative is to represent the trie in a single contiguous byte array as shown in Figure 1d. For each node, we store the node value, the size of the index, and the actual index as a list of alternating token IDs and byte offsets. Byte offsets are computed as the distance (in bytes) between the first byte of the child node and the first byte of its parent. The trie is represented in post-order because this is the most efficient way to write it out to a file during construction. For each node, we need to store the byte offsets of its children. When we write tries to file in post-order, this information is available by the time we need it. The only exception is the root node, whose offset is stored at the beginning of the file in a fixed-length field and updated at the very end.

This representation scheme has two advantages. First, since node references are represented as relative offsets within the array, the entire structure can be loaded or mapped (cf. Section 2.5) into memory without an explicit traversal. And secondly, it allows symbol-level compression of the structure with local, on-the-fly decompression as needed.

2.3 Trie compression by variable-length coding

Variable-length coding is a common technique for lossless compression of information. It exploits the uneven distribution of token frequencies in the underlying data, using short codes for frequently occurring symbols and long codes for infrequent symbols. Natural language data with its Zipfian distribution of token frequencies lends itself very well to variable-length coding. Instead of using more elaborate schemes such as Huffman (1952) coding, we simply assign token IDs in decreasing order of frequency. Each integer value is encoded as a sequence of digits in base-128 representation. Since the possible values of each digit (0–127) fit into 7 bits, the eighth bit in each byte is available as a flag bit to indicate whether or not more digits need to be read. Given the address of the first byte of a compressed integer representation, we know when to stop reading subsequent bytes/digits by looking at the flag bit.[2]

TPTs use two variants of this variable-length integer encoding, with different interpretations of the flag bit. For "stand-alone" values (node values, if they are integers, and the size of the index), the flag bit is set to 1 on the last digit of each number, and to 0 otherwise. When compressing node indices (i.e., the lists of child nodes and the respective arc labels), we use the flag bit on each byte to indicate whether the byte belongs to a key (token ID) or to a value (byte offset).

2.4 Binary search in compressed indices

In binary search in a sorted list of key-value pairs, we recursively cut the search range in half by choosing the midpoint of the current range as the new lower or upper bound, depending on whether the key at that point is less or greater than the search key. The recursion terminates when the search key is found or it has been determined that it is not in the list.

With compressed indices, it is not possible to determine the midpoint of the list precisely, because of the variable-length encoding of keys and values. However, the alternation of flag bits between keys and values in the index encoding allows us to recognize each byte in the index as either a 'key byte' or a 'value byte'. During search, we jump *approximately* to the middle of the search range and then scan bytes backwards until we encounter the beginning of a key, which will either be the byte at the very start of the index range or a byte with the flag bit set to '1' immediately preceded by a byte with the flag bit set to '0'. We then read the respective key and compare it against the search key.

2.5 Memory mapping

Memory mapping is a technique to provide fast file access through the OS-level paging mechanism. Memory mapping establishes a direct mapping between a file on disk and a region of virtual memory,

[2]This is a common technique for compact representation of non-negative integers. In the Perl world it is know as BER (Binary Encoded Representation) compressed integer format (see the chapter `perlpacktut` in the Perl documentation). Apache Lucene and Hadoop, among many other software projects, also define variable-length encoded integer types.

often by providing direct access to the kernel's file cache. Transfer from disk to memory and vice versa is then handled by the virtual memory manager; the program itself can access the file as if it was memory. There are several libraries that provide memory mapping interfaces; we used the *Boost Iostreams* C++ library.[3] One nice side-effect of memory mapping the entire structure is that we can relegate the decision as to when to fall back on disk to the operating system, without having to design and code our own page management system. As long as RAM is available, the data will reside in the kernel's file cache; as memory gets sparse, the kernel will start dropping pages and re-loading them from disk as needed. In a computer network, we can furthermore rely on the file server's file cache in addition to the individual host's file cache to speed up access.

2.6 Additional tweaks

In order to keep the trie representation as small as possible, we shift key values in the indices two bits to the left and pad them with two binary flags. One indicates whether or not a node value is actually stored on the respective child node. If this flag is set to 0, the node is assumed to have an externally defined default value. This is particularly useful for storing sequence counts. Due to the Zipfian distribution of frequencies in natural language data, the lower the count, the more frequent it is. If we define the threshold for storing counts as the default value, we don't need to store that value for all the sequences that barely meet the threshold.

The second flag indicates whether the node is terminal or whether it has children. Terminal nodes have no index, so we don't need to store the index size of 0 on these nodes. In fact, if the value of terminal nodes can be represented as an integer, we can store the node's value directly in the index of its parent and set the flag accordingly.

At search time, these flags are interpreted and the value shifted back prior to comparison with the search key.

To speed up search at the top level, the index at the root of the trie is implemented as an array of file offsets and flags, providing constant time access to top-level trie nodes.

[3] Available at `http://www.boost.org`.

3 Encoding node values

Information associated with each token sequence is stored directly in a compact format "on the node" in the TPT representation. Special reader functions convert the packed node value into whatever structure best represents the node value in memory. In this section, we discuss the encoding of node values for various sequence-based NLP databases, namely sequence count tables, language models, and phrase tables for SMT.

3.1 Count tables

The representation of count tables is straightforward: we represent the count as a compressed integer. For representing sequence co-occurrence counts (e.g., bilingual phrase co-occurrences), we concatenate the two sequences with a special marker (an extra token) at the concatenation point.

3.2 Back-off language models

Back-off language models (Katz, 1987) of order n define the conditional probability $\mathrm{P}(w_i \mid w_{i-n+1}^{i-1})$ recursively as follows.

$$\mathrm{P}(w_i \mid w_{i-n+1}^{i-1}) = \begin{cases} \bar{\mathrm{P}}(w_i \mid w_{i-n+1}^{i-1}) & \text{if found} \\ \beta(w_{i-n+1}^{i-1}) \cdot \bar{\mathrm{P}}(w_i \mid w_{i-n+2}^{i-1}) & \text{otherwise} \end{cases} \tag{1}$$

Here, $\bar{\mathrm{P}}(w_i \mid w_{i-n+1}^{i-1})$ is a smoothed estimate of $\mathrm{P}(w_i \mid w_{i-n+1}^{i-1})$, $\beta(w_{i-n+1}^{i-1})$ is the *back-off weight* (a kind of normalization constant), and w_{i-n+1}^{i-1} is a compact notation for the sequence $w_{i-n+1}, \ldots, w_{i-1}$.

In order to retrieve the value $\bar{\mathrm{P}}(w_i \mid w_{i-n+1}^{i-1})$, we have to retrieve up to n values from the data base. In the worst case, the language model contains no probability values $\bar{\mathrm{P}}(w_i \mid \text{context})$ for any context but back-off weights for all possible contexts up to length $n-1$. Since the contexts $w_{i-n+1}^{i-1}, \ldots, w_{i-1}^{i-1}$ have common suffixes, it is more efficient to organize the trie as a backwards suffix tree (Bell *et al.*, 1990), that is, to represent the context sequences in right-to-left order in the trie. On each node in the trie, we store the back-off weight for the respective context, and the list of possible successor words and their conditional probabilities. The SRI language modeling toolkit (Stolcke, 2002) organizes its trie structure in the same way.

Probability values and back-off weights are stored via value IDs that are assigned in decreasing order of value frequency in the model and encoded as compressed integers. The list of successor words and their probability IDs is represented in the same way as the nodes' indices, i.e., as a sorted list of $\langle$*word ID, probability value ID*$\rangle$ pairs in compressed format.

3.3 Phrase tables for SMT

Phrase tables for phrase-based SMT list for every source phrase a number of target phrases and for each phrase pair a number of numerical scores that are usually combined in a linear or log-linear model during translation.

To achieve a very compact representation of target phrases, we organize all target phrases in the table in a "bottom-up" trie: instead of storing on each node a list of arcs leading to children, we store the node's label and its parent. Each phrase can thus be represented by a single integer that gives the location of the leaf node; we can restore the respective phrase by following the path from the leaf to the root.

Phrase pair scores are entropy-encoded and stored with variable-length encoding. Since we have several entropy-encoded values to store for each phrase pair, and several phrases for each source phrase, we can achieve greater compression with optimally sized "bit blocks" instead of the octets we have used so far. By way of a historical accident, we are currently still using indicator bits on each bit block to indicate whether additional blocks need to be read; a more principled approach would have been to switch to proper Huffman (1952) coding. The optimal sizes of the bit blocks are calculated separately for each translation table prior to encoding and stored in the code book that maps from score IDs to actual scores.

4 Related work

The challenges of managing huge models have been addressed by a number of researchers in recent years.

4.1 Array offsets instead of memory pointers

The CMU-Cambridge language modeling toolkit (Clarkson and Rosenfeld, 1997) represents the context trie in contiguous arrays of fixed-size node records, where each array corresponds to a certain "layer" of the trie. Instead of memory pointers, links between nodes are represented by offsets into the respective array. With some additional bookkeeping, the toolkit manages to store array offsets in only 16 bits (see Whittaker and Raj (2001) for details). Quantization of probability values and back-off weights is used to reduce the amount of memory needed to store probability values and back-off weights (see Section 4.4 below).

4.2 Model filtering

Many research systems offer the option to filter the models at load time or offline, so that only information pertaining to tokens that occur in a given input is kept in memory; all other database entries are skipped. Language model implementations that offer model filtering at load time include the SRILM toolkit (Stolcke, 2002) and the *Portage* LM implementation (Badr *et al.*, 2007). For translation tables, the *Moses* system (Koehn *et al.*, 2007) as well as *Portage* offer model filtering (*Moses:* offline; *Portage:* offline and/or at load time). Model filtering requires that the input is known when the respective program is started and therefore is not feasible for server implementations.

4.3 On-demand loading

A variant of model filtering that is also viable for server implementations is on-demand loading. In the context of SMT, Zens and Ney (2007) store the phrase table on disk, represented as a trie with relative offsets, so that sections of the trie can be loaded into memory without rebuilding them. During translation, only those sections of the trie that actually match the input are loaded into memory. They report that their approach is "not slower than the traditional approach", which has a significant load time overhead. They do not provide a comparison of pure processing speed ignoring the initial table load time overhead of the "traditional approach".

IRSTLM (Federico and Cettolo, 2007) offers the option to use a custom page manager that relegates part of the structure to disk via memory-mapped files. The difference with our use of memory mapping is that IRSTLM still builds the structure in memory and then swaps part of it out to disk.

4.4 Lossy compression and pruning

Large models can also be reduced in size by lossy compression. Both SRILM and IRSTLM offer tools for language model pruning (Stolcke, 1998): if probability values for long contexts can be approximated well by the back-off computation, the respective entries are dropped.

Another form of lossy compression is the quantization of probability values and back-off weights. Whittaker and Raj (2001) use pruning, quantization and difference encoding to store language model parameters in as little as 4 bits per value, reducing language model sizes by to 60% with "minimal loss in recognition performance." Federico and Bertoldi (2006) show that the performance of an SMT system does not suffer if LM parameters are quantized into 256 distinct classes (8 bits per value).

Johnson *et al.* (2007) use significance tests to eliminate poor candidates from phrase tables for SMT. They are able to eliminate 90% of the phrase table entries without an adverse effect on translation quality.

Pruning and lossy compression are orthogonal to the approach taken in TPTs. The two approaches can be combined to achieve even more compact language models and phrase tables.

4.5 Hash functions

An obvious alternative to the use of trie structures is the use of hash functions that map from n-grams to slots containing associated information. With hash-based implementations, the keys are usually not stored at all in the database; hash collisions and therefore lookup errors are the price to be paid for compact storage. This risk can be controlled by the design of the hash function. Talbot and Brants (2008) show that Bloomier filters (Chazelle *et al.*, 2004) can be used to create perfect hash functions for language models. This guarantees that there are no collisions between existing entries in the database but does not eliminate the risk of false positives for items that are not in the database.

For situations where space is at a premium and speed negotiable (e.g., in interactive context-based spelling correction, where the number of lookups is not in the range of thousands or millions per second), Church *et al.* (2007) present a compressed trigram model that combines Stolcke (1998) pruning with Golomb (1966) coding of inter-arrival times in the (sparse) range of hash values computed by the hash function. One major drawback of their method of storage is that search is linear in the total number of keys in the worst case (usually mediated by auxiliary data structures that cache information).

Since hash-based implementations of token sequence-based NLP databases usually don't store the search keys, it is not possible to iterate through such databases.

4.6 Distributed implementations

Brants *et al.* (2007) present an LM implementation that distributes very large language models over a network of language model servers. The delay due to network latency makes it inefficient to issue individual lookup requests to distributed language models. As Brants *et al.* point out: "Onboard memory is around 10,000 times faster" than access via the network. Instead, requests are batched and sent to the server in chunks of 1,000 or 10,000 requests.

5 Experiments

We present here the results of empirical evaluations of the effectiveness of TPTs for encoding n-gram language models and phrase tables for SMT. We have also used TPTs to encode n-gram count databases such as the Google 1T web n-gram database (Brants and Franz, 2006), but are not able to provide detailed results within the space limitations of this paper.[4]

5.1 Perplexity computation with 5-gram language models

We compared the performance of TPT-encoded language models against three other language model implementations: the SRI language modeling toolkit (Stolcke, 2002), IRSTLM (Federico and Cettolo, 2007), and the language model implementation currently used in the *Portage* SMT system (Badr *et al.*, 2007), which uses a pointer-based implementation but is able to perform fast LM filtering at load time. The task was to compute the perplexity of a text of

[4]Bottom line: the entire Google 1T web n-gram data base fits into about 16 GB (file/virtual memory), compared to 24 GB as *gzip*-compressed text files (file only).

Table 1: Memory use and runtimes of different LM implementations on a perplexity computation task.

		file/mem. size (GB)				1st run (times in sec.)					2nd run (times in sec.)				
		file	virt.	real	b/ng[1]	ttfr[2]	wall	usr	sys	cpu	ttfr	wall	usr	sys	cpu
full model loaded	**SRILM[3]**	5.2	16.3	15.3	42.2	940	1136	217	31	21%	846	1047	215	30	23%
	SRILM-C[4]	5.2	13.0	12.9	33.6	230	232	215	14	98%	227	229	213	14	98%
	IRST	5.1	5.5	5.4	14.2	614	615	545	13	90%	553	555	544	11	100%
	IRST-m[5]	5.1	5.5	1.6	14.2	548	744	545	8	74%	547	549	544	5	100%
	IRST-Q[6]	3.1	3.5	3.4	9.1	588	589	545	9	93%	551	553	544	8	100%
	IRST-Qm	3.1	3.5	1.4	9.1	548	674	546	7	81%	548	549	544	5	99%
	Portage	8.0	10.5	10.5	27.2	120	**122**	90	15	85%	110	112	90	14	92%
	TPT	**2.9**	**3.4**	**1.4**	**7.5**	**2**	127	**2**	2	**2%**	**1**	**2**	**1**	**1**	98%
filtered[7]	**SRILM**	5.2	6.0	5.9		111	112	90	12	91%	99	99	90	9	99%
	SRILM-C	5.2	4.6	4.5		112	113	93	11	91%	100	105	93	8	99%
	Portage	8.0	4.5	4.4		120	122	75	11	70%	80	81	74	7	99%

Notes: [1] **B**ytes per **n**-**g**ram (Amount of virtual memory used divided by total number of n-grams). [2] **T**ime **t**o **f**irst **r**esponse (first value returned). This was measured in a separate experiment, so the times reported sometimes do not match those in the other columns exactly. [3] Node indices stored in hashes. [4] "Compact" mode: node indices stored in sorted arrays instead of hashes. [5] Uses a custom paging mechanism to reduce memory requirements; [6] Values are quantized into 256 discrete classes, so that each value can be stored in 1 byte. [7] Models filtered on evaluation text at load time.

Table 2: Language model statistics.

	Gigaword	Hansard
unigrams	8,135,668	211,055
bigrams	47,159,160	4,045,363
trigrams	116,206,275	6,531,550
4-grams	123,297,762	9,776,573
5-grams	120,416,442	9,712,384
file size (ARPA format)	14.0 GB	1.1 GB
file size (ARPA .gz)	3.7 GB	225 MB

10,000 lines (275,000 tokens) with a 5-gram language model trained on the English Gigaword corpus (Graff, 2003). Some language model statistics are given in Table 2.

We measured memory use and total run time in two runs: the first run was with an empty OS-level file cache, forcing the system to read all data from the hard disk. The second run was immediately after the first run, utilizing whatever information was still cached by the operating system. All experiments were run successively on the same 64-bit machine with 16 GB of physical memory.[5] In order to eliminate distortions by variances in the network and file server load at the time the experiments were run, only locally mounted disks were used.

The results of the comparison are shown in Table 1. SRILM has two modi operandi: one uses hashes to access child nodes in the underlying trie implementation, the other one (SRILM-C) sorted arrays. The "faster" hash-based implementation pushes the architecture beyond its limitations: the system starts thrashing and is therefore the slowest by a wide margin.

The most significant bottleneck in the TPT implementation is disk access delay. Notice the huge difference in run-time between the first and the second run. In the first run, CPU utilization is merely 2%: the program is idle most of the time, waiting for the data from disk. In the second run, the file is still completely in the system's file cache and is available immediately. When processing large amounts of data in parallel on a cluster, caching on the cluster's file server will benefit all users of the respective model, once a particular page has been requested for the first time by any of them.

Another nice feature of the TPT implementation is the short delay between starting the program and being able to perform the first lookup: the first n-gram probability is available after only 2 seconds.

The slightly longer wall time of TPLMs ("tightly packed language models") in comparison to the *Portage* implementation is due to the way the data file is read: *Portage* reads it sequentially, while TPLMs request the pages in more or less random order, resulting in slightly less efficient disk access.

[5]Linux kernel version 2.6.18 (SUSE) on an Intel® Xeon® 2.33 GHz processor with 4 MB cache.

Table 3: Model load times and translation speed for batch translation with the *Portage* SMT system.

# of sentences per batch	Baseline			TPPT + Baseline LM			TPLM + Baseline PT			TPPT + TPLM		
	load time	w/s[1]	w/s[2]	load time	w/s[1]	w/s[2]	load time	w/s[1]	w/s[2]	load time[3]	w/s[1]	w/s[2]
47	210s	5.4	2.4	16s	5.0	4.6	178s	5.9	2.67	< 1s	5.5	5.5
10	187s	5.5	0.8	16s	5.1	3.6	170s	5.6	0.91	< 1s	5.6	5.6
1	—	—	—	15s	5.0	1.0	154s	5.5	0.12	< 1s	5.3	5.2

Baseline: *Portage*'s implementation as pointer structure with load-time filtering.
TP: Tightly packed; **PT:** phrase table; **LM:** language model
[1] words per second, excluding load time (pure translation time after model loading)
[2] words per second, including load time (bottom line translation speed)

5.2 TPTs in statistical machine translation

To test the usefulness of TPTs in a more realistic setting, we integrated them into the *Portage* SMT system (Sadat *et al.*, 2005) and ran large-scale translations in parallel batch processes on a cluster. Both language models and translation tables were encoded as TPTs and compared against the native *Portage* implementation. The system was trained on ca. 5.2 million parallel sentences from the Canadian Hansard (English: 101 million tokens; French: 113 million tokens). The language model statistics are given in Table 2; the phrase table contained about 60.6 million pairs of phrases up to length 8. The test corpus of 1134 sentences was translated from English into French in batches of 1, 10, and 47 or 48 sentences.[6]

Translation tables were not pre-filtered a priori to contain only entries matching the input. Pre-filtered tables are smaller and therefore faster to read, which is advantageous when the same text is translated repeatedly; the set-up we used more closely resembles a system in production that has to deal with unknown input. *Portage* does, however, filter models at load time to reduce memory use. The total (real) memory use for translations was between 1 and 1.2 GB, depending on the batch job, for all systems.

Table 3 shows the run-time test results. Ignoring model load times, the processing speed of the current *Portage* implementation and TPTs is comparable. However, when we take into account load times (which must be taken into account under realistic conditions), the advantages of the TPT implementation become evident.

[6]The peculiar number 47/48 is the result of using the default batch size used in minimum error rate training of the system in other experiments.

6 Conclusions

We have presented Tightly Packed Tries, a compact implementation of trie structures for NLP databases that provide a good balance between compactness and speed. They are only slightly (if at all) slower but require much less memory than pointer-based implementations. Extensive use of the memory-mapping mechanism provides very short load times and allows memory sharing between processes. Unlike solutions that are custom-tailored to specific models (e.g., trigram language models), TPTs provide a general strategy for encoding all types of NLP databases that rely on token sequences for indexing information. The novelty in our approach lies in the compression of the indexing structure itself, not just of the associated information. While the underlying mechanisms are well-known, we are not aware of any work so far that combines them to achieve fast-loading, compact and fast data structures for large-scale NLP applications.

References

Badr, G., E. Joanis, S. Larkin, and R. Kuhn. 2007. "Manageable phrase-based statistical machine translation models." *5th Intl. Conf. on Computer Recognition Systems (CORES)*. Wroclaw, Poland.

Bell, T. C., J. G. Cleary, and I. H. Witten. 1990. *Text Compression*. Prentice Hall.

Brants, T. and A. Franz. 2006. "Web 1T 5-gram Version 1." LDC Catalogue Number LDC2006T13.

Brants, T., A. C. Popat, P. Xu, F. J. Och, and J. Dean. 2007. "Large language models in machine translation." *EMNLP-CoNLL 2007*, 858–867. Prague, Czech Republic.

Chazelle, B., J. Kilian, R. Rubinfeld, and A. Tal. 2004. "The Bloomier filter: An efficient data structure for static support lookup tables." *15th Annual ACM-SIAM Symposium on Discrete Algorithms*. New Orleans, LA, USA.

Church, K., T. Hart, and J. Gao. 2007. "Compressing trigram language models with Golomb coding." *EMNLP-CoNLL 2007*, 199–207. Prague, Czech Republic.

Clarkson, P. R. and R. Rosenfeld. 1997. "Statistical language modeling using the CMU-Cambridge toolkit." *EUROSPEECH 1997*, 2707–2710. Rhodes, Greece.

Federico, M. and N. Bertoldi. 2006. "How many bits are needed to store probabilities for phrase-based translation?" *Workshop on Statistical Machine Translation*, 94–101. New York City.

Federico, M. and M. Cettolo. 2007. "Efficient handling of n-gram language models for statistical machine translation." *Second Workshop on Statistical Machine Translation*, 88–95. Prague, Czech Republic.

Fredkin, E. 1960. "Trie memory." *Communications of the ACM*, 3(9):490–499.

Golomb, S. W. 1966. "Run-length encodings." *IEEE Transactions on Information Theory*, 12(3):399–401.

Graff, D. 2003. "English Gigaword." LDC Catalogue Number LDC2003T05.

Huffman, D. A. 1952. "A method for the construction of minimum-redundancy codes." *Proceedings of the IRE*, 40(9):1098–1102. Reprinted in *Resonance* 11(2).

Johnson, H., J. Martin, G. Foster, and R. Kuhn. 2007. "Improving translation quality by discarding most of the phrasetable." *EMNLP-CoNLL 2007*, 967–975. Prague, Czech Republic.

Katz, S. M. 1987. "Estimation of probabilities from sparse data for the language model component of a speech recognizer." *IEEE Transactions on Acoustics, Speech, and Signal Processing*, 35(3):400–401.

Koehn, P., H. Hoang, A. Birch, C. Callison-Burch, M. Federico, N. Bertoldi, B. Cowan, W. Shen, C. Moran, R. Zens, C. Dyer, O. Bojar, A. Constantin, and E. Herbst. 2007. "Moses: Open source toolkit for statistical machine translation." *ACL 2007 Demonstration Session*. Prague, Czech Republic.

Sadat, F., H. Johnson, A. Agbago, G. Foster, R. Kuhn, J. Martin, and A. Tikuisis. 2005. "PORTAGE: A phrase-based machine translation system." *ACL Workshop on Building and Using Parallel Texts*, 133–136. Ann Arbor, MI, USA. Also available as NRC-IIT publication NRC-48525.

Stolcke, A. 1998. "Entropy-based pruning of backoff language models." *DARPA Broadcast News Transcription and Understanding Workshop*, 270–274. Lansdowne, VA, USA.

Stolcke, A. 2002. "SRILM — an extensible language modeling toolkit." *Intl. Conf. on Spoken Language Processing*. Denver, CO, USA.

Talbot, D. and T. Brants. 2008. "Randomized language models via perfect hash functions." *ACL 2008*, 505–513. Columbus, Ohio.

Whittaker, E. W. D. and B. Raj. 2001. "Quantization-based language model compression." *EUROSPEECH 2001*, 33–36. Aalborg, Denmark.

Zens, R. and H. Ney. 2007. "Efficient phrase-table representation for machine translation with applications to online MT and speech translation." *NAACL-HLT 2007 2007*, 492–499. Rochester, New York.

Scaling up a NLU system from text to dialogue understanding

R. Delmonte, A. Bristot, G. Voltolina
Department of Language Science -
Università Ca' Foscari - 30123 -
VENEZIA
delmont@unive.it

Vincenzo Pallotta
Webster University, Geneva
Switzerland
pallotta@webster.ch

Abstract

In this paper we will present work carried out to scale up the system for text understanding called GETARUNS, and port it to be used in dialogue understanding. We will present the adjustments we made in order to cope with transcribed spoken dialogues like those produced in the ICSI Berkely project. In a final section we present preliminary evaluation of the system on non-referential pronominals individuation.

1 Introduction

Very much like other deep linguistic processing systems (see Allen et al.), our system is a generic text/dialogue understanding system that can be used in connection with an ontology – WordNet - and/or a repository of commonsense knowledge like CONCEPTNET. Word sense disambiguation takes place at the level of semantic interpretation and is represented in the Discourse Model.

Computing semantic representations for spoken dialogues is a particularly hard task which – when compared to written text processing - requires the following additional information to be made available:

- adequate treatment of fragments;
- adequate treatment of short turns, in particular one-word turns;
- adequate treatment of first person singular and plural pronominal expressions;
- adequate treatment of disfluencies, thus including cases of turns made up of just such expressions, or cases when they are found inside the utterance;
- adequate treatment of overlaps;
- adequate treatment of speaker identity for pronominal coreference;

In our system, then, every dialogue turn receives one polarity label, indicating negativity or positivity, and this is computed by looking into a dictionary of polarity items. This is subsequently used to decide on argumentative automatic classification.

The Berkeley ICSI dialogues are characterized by the need to argument in a exhaustive manner the topics to be debated which are the theme of each multiparty dialogue. The mean length of utterances/turns in each dialogue we parsed was rather long.

2 The System GETARUNS

GETARUNS[1], the system for text understanding developed at the University of Venice, is organized as a pipeline which includes two versions of the system: what we call the Partial and the Deep GETARUNS (Delmonte 2007;2009). The Deep version is equipped with three main modules: a lower module for parsing, where sentence strategies are implemented; a middle module for semantic interpretation and discourse model construction which is cast into Situation Semantics; and a higher module where reasoning and generation takes place.

2.1 The Algorithm for Overlaps

Overlaps are an important component of all spoken dialogue analysis. In all dialogue transcription, overlaps are treated as a separate turn from the one in which they occur, which usually follows it. On the contrary, when computing overlaps we set as our first goal that of recovering the temporal order. This is done because overlaps may introduce linguistic elements which influence the local context. Eventually, they may determine the interpretation of the current utterance.

[1] The system has been tested in STEP competition, and can be downloaded at, http://project.cgm.unive.it/html/sharedtask/.

Proceedings of the NAACL HLT Workshop on Software Engineering, Testing, and Quality Assurance for Natural Language Processing, pages 40–41,
Boulder, Colorado, June 2009.

For these reasons, they cannot be moved to a separate turn because they must be semantically interpreted where they temporally belong.
The algorithm we built looks at time stamps, and everytime the following turn begins at a time preceding the ending time of current turn it enters a special recursive procedure. It looks for internal interruption in the current turn and splits the utterance where the interruption occurs. Then it parses it split initial portion of current utterance and continues with the overlapping turn. This may be reiterated in case another overlap follows which again begins before the end of current utterance. Eventually, it returns to the analysis of the current turn with the remaining portion of current utterance.

2.2 The Treatment of Fragments and Short Turns

Fragments and short turns are filtered by a lexical lookup procedure that searches for specific linguistic elements which are part of a list of backchannels, acknowledgements expressions and other similar speech acts. In case this procedure has success, no further computation takes place. However, this only applies to utterances shorter than 5 words, and should be made up only of such special words. No other linguistic element should be present apart from non-words, that is words which are only partially produced and have been transcribed with a dash at the end. Otherwise we proceed as follows:
- graceful failure procedures for ungrammatical sentences, which might be fullfledged utterances but semantically uninterpretable due to the presence of repetitions, false starts and similar disfluency phenomena. Or else they may be just fragments, i.e. partial or incomplete utterances, hence non-interpretable as such; this is done by imposing grammatical constraints of wellformedness in the parser.
We implemented a principled treatment of elliptical utterances and contribute one specific speech act. They may express agreement/ disagreement, acknowledgements, assessments, continuers etc. All these items are computed as being complements of abstract verb SAY which is introduced in the analysis, and has as subject, the name of current speaker.

3 The Experiment

We set up an experiment in order to test the new version of the system, that is detecting referential from nonreferential uses of personal pronouns "you", "we" and "it".
In order to take decisions as to whether pronouns are to be interpreted as referential or not a recursive procedure checks the type of governing predicate. Referential pronouns are then passed on to the pronominal binding algorithm that looks for local antecedents if any. Otherwise, the pronouns is labeled as having External coreference in the previous discourse stretch. The Anaphora Resolution module will then take care of the antecedent and a suitable semantic identifier will be associated to it. On the contrary, if the pronouns are judged to be referentially empty or generic, no binding takes place. Here below is a table containing total values for pronouns WE/YOU/IT in all the 10 dialogues analysed.

	Referential	Generic	Total
WE	1186	706	1892
YOU	1045	742	1787
IT	1593	1008	2601
Total	3824	2456	6280

Table 1. Overall count of pronominal expressions

Results for the experiment are as follows

	Recall	Precision	F-Score
WE	98.2%	60.59%	74.94%
YOU	99.3%	70.99%	82.79%
IT	97.6%	64.2%	77.45%

Table 2. Results for pronominal expressions

References

Allen, J., M. Dzikovska, M. Manshadi, and M. Swift. 2007. Deep linguistic processing for spoken dialogue systems. In ACL 2007 Workshop on Deep Linguistic Processing, pp. 49–56.

Delmonte R. 2007. *Computational Linguistic Text Processing – Logical Form, Semantic Interpretation, Discourse Relations and Question Answering*, Nova Science Publishers, New York.

Delmonte R. 2009. *Computational Linguistic Text Processing – Lexicon, Grammar, Parsing and Anaphora Resolution*, Nova Science Publishers, New York.

Towards Agile and Test-Driven Development in NLP Applications

Jana Z. Sukkarieh
Educational Testing Service
Rosedale Road
Princeton, NJ 08541, USA
Jsukkarieh@ets.org

Jyoti Kamal
Educational Testing Service
Rosedale Road
Princeton, NJ 08541, USA
Jkamal@ets.org

Abstract

c-rater® is the Educational Testing Service technology for automatic content scoring for short free-text responses. In this paper, we contend that an Agile and test-driven development environment optimizes the development of an NLP-based technology.

1 Introduction

c-rater (Leacock and Chodorow, 2003) is the Educational Testing Service technology for the automatic content scoring of short free-text responses for items whose rubrics are concept-based. This means that a set of concepts or main points are prespecified in the rubric (see the example in Table 1). We view c-rater's task as a textual entailment problem that involves the detection of whether a student's answer entails a particular concept (with the additional challenge that the students' data contains misspellings and grammatical errors). Our solution depends on a combination of rule-based and statistically-based NLP modules (Sukkarieh and Blackmore, 2009). In addition to databases, a JBOSS server (www.jboss.org), and two user interfaces, c-rater consists of 10 modules–eight of which are Natural Language Processing (NLP) modules. Figure 1 depicts the system's architecture. The c-rater engine is where all the linguistic processing and concept detection takes place. Section 2 lists some of the major problems we face while developing such a complex NLP-based application and how our adoption of Agile and test-driven development is helping us.

Example Item (Full Credit 2)	***Concepts or main/key points:***
Figures are given ***Prompt:*** The figures show three polygons. Is the polygon in Figure 1 an octagon, hexagon, or parallelogram? Explain your answer.	**C1:** *The polygon/it is a quadrilateral with two sets of parallel sides OR the opposite sides are of equal length OR opposite angles are equal* **C2:** *The polygon/it has four/4 sides*
Scoring rules: 2 points for C1 (only if C2 is not present) 1 point for C1 and C2 Otherwise 0	

Table 1. Example item for c-rater scoring

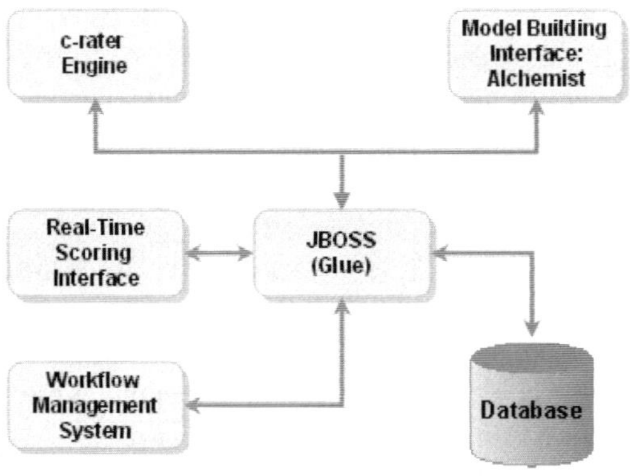

Figure 1. c-rater's System Architecture

2 Major Concerns and Solutions

2.1 Communication

In the past, the implementation of each module was done in isolation and communication among team members was lacking. When a team member

Proceedings of the NAACL HLT Workshop on Software Engineering, Testing, and Quality Assurance for Natural Language Processing, pages 42–44, Boulder, Colorado, June 2009. ©2009 Association for Computational Linguistics

encountered a problem, it was only then that s/he would be aware of some logic or data structure changes by another member. This is not necessarily an NLP-specific problem, however due to the particularly frequent modifications in NLP-based applications (see Section 2.2), communication is more challenging and updates are even more crucial. The adoption of Scrum within Agile (Augustine, 2005) has improved communication tremendously. Although both the task backlog and the choice of tasks within each sprint is done by the product owner, throughout the sprint the planning, requirement analysis, design, coding, and testing is performed by all of the team members. This has been effecting in decreasing the number of logic design errors.

2.2 Planning and Frequent Modification

Very frequent modifications and re-prioritizing are, to a great extent, due to the nature of NL input and constant re-specification, extension, and customization of NLP modules. This could also be due to changes in business requirements, e.g. to tailor the needs of the application to a particular client's needs. Further, this could be a response to emerging research, following a sudden intuition or performing a heuristic approach. Agile takes care of all these issues. It allows the development to adapt to changes more quickly and retract/replace the last feature-based enhancement(s) when the need arises. It allows for incorporating research time and experimental studies into the task backlog; hence the various sprints. The nature of the Agile environment allows us also to add tasks driven by the business needs and consider them highest in value.

2.3 Metrics for Functionality and Progress

Metrics for functionality includes measuring progress, comparing one version to another and monitoring the effect of frequent modifications. This particularly proves challenging due to the nature of c-rater's tasks and the NLP modules. In most software, the business value is a working product. In c-rater, it is not only about producing a score but producing one for the "right" reasons and not due to errors in the linguistic features obtained.

Until recently, comparing versions meant comparing holistic scores without a sense of the effect of particular changes. Evaluating the effect of a change often meant hand-checking hundreds and hundreds of cases. To improve monitoring, we have designed an engine test suite (each is a pair <model-sentence, answer> where model-sentence is a variant of a concept) and introduced automated testing. The suite is categorized according to the linguistic phenomenon of interest (e.g., passive, ergative, negation, appositive, parser output, co-reference output). Some categories follow the phenomena in Vanderwende and Dolan (2006). Some RTE data was transformed for engine tests. This produced a finer-grained view of the NLP modules performance, decreased the amount of hand-checking, and increased our confidence about the "correctness" of our scores.

2.4 Maintenance and Debugging

Until very recently maintaining and debugging the system was very challenging. We faced many issues including the unsystematic scattering of common data structures, making it hard to manage dependencies; long functions making it difficult to track bugs; and late integration or lack of regular updates causing, at times, the system to crash or not compile. Although this may not be deemed NLP-specific, the need to modify NLP modules more frequently than anticipated has made this particularly challenging. To face this challenge, we introduced unit tests (UT) and continuous integration. We usually select some representative or "typical" NL input for certain phenomena, create an expected output, create a *failed* UT, and make it pass. An additional challenge is that since students' responses are noisy, sometimes choosing "typical" text is hard. Ideally, unit tests are supposed to be written before or at the same time as the code; we were able to do that for approximately 40% of the code. The rest of the unit testing was being written after the code was written. For legacy code, we have covered around 10-20% of the code.

In conclusion, we strongly believe like Degerstedt and Jönsson (2006), Agile and Test-Driven Development form a most-suitable environment for building NLP-based applications.

Acknowledgments

Special thanks to Kenneth Willian, and Rene Lawless.

References

Augustine, S. Managing Agile Projects. 2005. Published by Prentice Hall Professional Technical Reference. ISBN 0131240714, 9780131240711. 229 pages.

Degerstedt, L. and Jönsson, A. 2006. *LINTest, A development tool for testing dialogue systems.* In: Proceedings of the 9th International Conference on Spoken Language Processing (Interspeech/ICSLP), Pittsburgh, USA, pp. 489-492.

Leacock, C. and Chodorow, M. 2003. *C-rater: Automated Scoring of Short-Answer Question.* Journal of Computers and Humanities. pp. 389-405.

Sukkarieh, J. Z., & Blackmore, J. To appear. *c-rater: Automatic Content Scoring for Short Constructed Responses.* To appear in the Proceedings of the 22nd International Conference for the Florida Artificial Intelligence Research Society, Florida, USA, May 2009.

Vanderwende, L. and Dolan, W. B. 2006. *What Syntax Can Contribute in the Entailment Task.* J. Quinonero-Candela et al. (eds.). Machine Learning Challenges, Lecture notes in computer science, pp. 205-216. Springer Berlin/Heidelberg.

Grammar Engineering for CCG using Ant and XSLT*

Scott Martin, Rajakrishnan Rajkumar, and Michael White
Ohio State University
Department of Linguistics
{scott,raja,mwhite}@ling.ohio-state.edu

Overview

Corpus conversion and grammar extraction have traditionally been portrayed as tasks that are performed once and never again revisited (Burke et al., 2004). We report the successful implementation of an approach to these tasks that facilitates the improvement of grammar engineering as an evolving process. Taking the standard version of the CCGbank (Hockenmaier and Steedman, 2007) as input, our system then introduces greater depth of linguistic insight by augmenting it with attributes the original corpus lacks: Propbank roles and head lexicalization for case-marking prepositions (Boxwell and White, 2008), derivational re-structuring for punctuation analysis (White and Rajkumar, 2008), named entity annotation and lemmatization. Our implementation applies successive XSLT transforms controlled by Apache Ant (`http://ant.apache.org/`) to an XML translation of this corpus, finally producing an OpenCCG grammar (`http://openccg.sourceforge.net/`). This design is beneficial to grammar engineering both because of XSLT's unique suitability to performing arbitrary transformations of XML trees and the fine-grained control that Ant provides. The resulting system enables state-of-the-art BLEU scores for surface realization on section 23 of the CCGbank.

1 Design

Rather than transforming the corpus, it would be simple to introduce several of the corpus augmentations that we make (e.g. punctuation restructuring) during grammar extraction. However, machine learning applications (e.g., realization ranking) benefit when the corpus and extracted grammar are consistent. A case in point: annotating the corpus with named entities, then using n-gram models with words replaced by their class labels to score realization.

Accordingly, our pipeline design starts by generating an XML version of the CCGbank using JavaCC (`http://javacc.dev.java.net/`) from the original corpus. Next, conversion and extraction transforms are applied to create a converted corpus (also in XML) and extracted grammar (in OpenCCG format).

We refactored our original design to separate the grammar engineering task into several configurable processes using Ant tasks. This simplifies process management, speeds experiment iterations, and facilitates the comparison of different grammar engineering strategies.

2 Implementation

It seemed natural to implement our pipeline procedure in XSLT since both OpenCCG grammars and our CCGbank translation are represented in XML. Aside from its inherent attributes, XSLT requires no re-compilation as a result of being an interpreted language. Also, because both conversion and extraction use a series of transforms in a chain, each required sub-step can be split into as many XSLT transforms as desired.

Both the conversion and extraction steps were implemented by extending Ant with custom tasks as configuring Ant tasks requires no

*This work was supported in part by NSF grant no. IIS-0812297.

Proceedings of the NAACL HLT Workshop on Software Engineering, Testing, and Quality Assurance for Natural Language Processing, pages 45–46,
Boulder, Colorado, June 2009.

source editing or compilation. Ant is particularly well-suited to this process because, like OpenCCG (whose libraries are used in the extraction phase), it is written in Java. Our system also employs the Ant-provided `javacc` task, invoking the JavaCC parser to translate the CCGbank to XML. This approach is preferable to a direct Java implementation because it keeps source code and configuration separate, allowing for more rapid grammar engineering iterations.

Our particular implementation harnesses Ant's built-in `FileSet` (for specification of groups of corpus files) and `FileList` (for reuse of series of XSLT transforms) data types. The first of our extension tasks, `convert`, encapsulates the conversion process while the second task, `extract`, implements the grammar extraction procedure for a previously-converted corpus.

3 Experimental Impact

Our conversion process currently supports various experiments by including only specified transforms. We gain the ability to create corpora with various combinations of attributes, among them punctuation annotation, semantic class information, and named entities (lack of space precludes inclusion of examples here; see `http://www.ling.ohio-state.edu/~scott/publications/grammareng/`). In addition to extracting grammars, the extraction task employs a constrained parser to create logical forms (LFs) for surface realization and extracts SRILM training data for realization scoring. This task also enables feature extraction from LF graphs for training during supertagging for realization (Espinosa et al., 2008).

Our design supports comprehensive experimentation and has helped facilitate recent efforts to investigate factors impacting surface realization, such as semantic classes and named entities. Our initial results reported in (White et al., 2007) record 69.7% single-rooted LFs with a BLEU score of 0.5768. But current figures stand at 95.8% single-rooted LFs and a state-of-the art BLEU score of 0.8506 on section 23 of the CCGbank. (Fragmentary LFs result when at least one semantic dependency is missing from the LF graph.) In achieving these results, improvements in the grammar engineering process have been at least as important as improvements in the statistical models.

4 Conclusions and Future Work

We designed and implemented a system that facilitates the process of grammar engineering by separating conversion and extraction steps into a pipeline of XSLT transforms. Our Ant implementation is highly configurable and has positive effects on our grammar engineering efforts, including increased process control and a shortened testing cycle for different grammar engineering approaches. Future work will focus on increasing the number of single-rooted LFs and integrating this system with OpenCCG.

References

[Boxwell and White2008] Stephen Boxwell and Michael White. 2008. Projecting Propbank roles onto the CCGbank. In *Proc. LREC-08.*

[Burke et al.2004] Michael Burke, Aoife Cahill, Mairead Mccarthy, Ruth O'Donovan, Josef Genabith, and Andy Way. 2004. Evaluating automatic LFG F-structure annotation for the Penn-II treebank. *Research on Language and Computation*, 2:523–547, December.

[Espinosa et al.2008] Dominic Espinosa, Michael White, and Dennis Mehay. 2008. Hypertagging: Supertagging for surface realization with CCG. In *Proc. ACL-08: HLT.*

[Hockenmaier and Steedman2007] Julia Hockenmaier and Mark Steedman. 2007. CCGbank: A Corpus of CCG Derivations and Dependency Structures Extracted from the Penn Treebank. *Computational Linguistics*, 33(3):355–396.

[White and Rajkumar2008] Michael White and Rajakrishnan Rajkumar. 2008. A more precise analysis of punctuation for broad-coverage surface realization with CCG. In *Proc. of the Workshop on Grammar Engineering Across Frameworks (GEAF08).*

[White et al.2007] Michael White, Rajakrishnan Rajkumar, and Scott Martin. 2007. Towards broad coverage surface realization with CCG. In *Proc. of the Workshop on Using Corpora for NLG: Language Generation and Machine Translation (UC-NLG+MT).*

Web Service Integration for Next Generation Localisation

David Lewis, Stephen Curran, Kevin Feeney, Zohar Etzioni, John Keeney
Andy Way
Reinhard Schäler

Centre for Next Generation Localisation

Knowledge and Data Engineering Group
Trinity College Dublin, Ireland
{Dave.Lewis|Stephen.curran|Kevin.Feeney|etzioniz|John.Keeney}@cs.tcd.ie

School of Computing
Dublin City University, Ireland
away@computing.dcu.ie

Centre for Localisation Research
University of Limerick, Ireland
Reinhard.Schaler@ul.ie

Abstract

Developments in Natural Language Processing technologies promise a variety of benefits to the localization industry, both in its current form in performing bulk enterprise-based localization and in the future in supporting personalized web-based localization on increasingly user-generated content. As an increasing variety of natural language processing services become available, it is vital that the localization industry employs the flexible software integration techniques that will enable it to make best use of these technologies. To date however, the localization industry has been slow reap the benefits of modern integration technologies such as web service integration and orchestration. Based on recent integration experiences, we examine how the localization industry can best exploit web-based integration technologies in developing new services and exploring new business models

1 Introduction

Research and development of natural language processing technologies are leading to a variety of advances in areas such as text analytics and machine translation that have a range of commercial applications. The Localization Industry in particular, is strategically well placed to make good use of these advances as it faces the challenge of localizing accelerating volumes of digital content that is being targeted at increasingly global markets of this content. It needs to exploit the benefits of NLP technologies to reduce the cost of translation and minimise the time to market of this digital content. Furthermore, where the localization industry best learns how to efficiently and flexibly employ NLP technologies in the localization of digital content it will be ideally placed to develop new services and exploit new business opportunities offered by the WWW. In particular, today's localization techniques are not able to keep pace with the WWW's ability to dynamically compose and personalize existing content and to support rapid development of large volumes of user generated content. To meet this challenge, localization processes must effectively employ NLP to move from manually centered, professional batch activities to highly automated, highly participative continuous activities. To do this, the technologies of the WWW need to be employed to dynamically combine NLP technologies and leverage different levels of human linguistic abilities and knowledge to best accomplish the task at hand.

In this paper we examine how this vision, which we term *Next Generation Localization*, can be supported by current web-based, service-oriented software integration techniques such as web service integration and orchestration. Based on recent integration experience we review the current issues in using open interoperability standards and web services to the integration of commercial localization platforms and NLP software. We then describe some generic definitions for NLP web services and how these provide flexibility in developing new localization service compositions. Finally, we outline the major software integration challenges facing the localization industry and describe how these are being addressed at Ireland's Centre for Next Generation Localization (CNGL).

2 Next Generation Localization

Traditional localization technologies and workflows are no longer able to cope with the escalating growth in volume. Traditional localization methods are not adequate to manage, localize and personalize unpredictable, on-line, multilingual, digital content. Machine Translation (MT) needs to be integrated into translation and post-editing workflows together with human translators. Novel machine-learning-based language technologies can automatically provide metadata annotations (labels) to localization input in order to automate localization standardization and management.

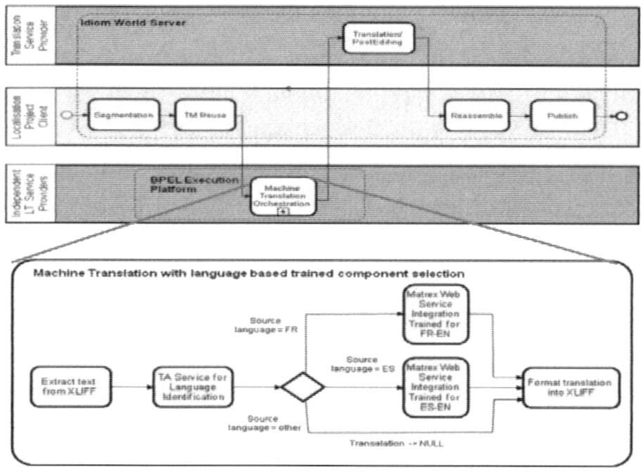

Figure 1: Example use of Web Service Orchestration in a Localisation Workflow

For Next Generation Localisation to be achieved, the individual components need to be interoperable and easily reconfigurable. The complexity of the resulting systems poses substantial software engineering challenges and crucially requires detailed user requirement studies, technical and user interface standards, as well as support for rapid prototyping and formative evaluation early on in the software lifecycle. Blueprints for an industrial environment for Next Generation Localisation, which we term a *Localisation Factory*, are needed to guide the development of localisation services systems integrating advanced language, digital content and localisation management technologies. However, in order to successfully achieve the goal of technical interoperability these services crucially needs to be supplemented by standardised localisation processes and workflows for the Localisation Factory. Figure 1 gives an overview of a typical localisation workflow, that would be used for translating the content such as the use manual for a product, into multiple languages for different target markets. Typically this involves segmenting the content into sentences, looking up previously translated sentences from a Translation Memory (MT), before passing untranslated segments to a Machine Translation (TM) service to generate further candidate translations. Next, the job is passed to professional translators, who can accept automated translations or provide their own translations. Current practice in performing such workflows uses localisation platforms such as SDL's Idiom WorldServer to integrate Translation Memory databases, Machine Translation packages and the routing of jobs to translators who typically work remotely under the management of a localisation service provision agency.

The localization industry has already undertaken a number of separate standardization activities to support interoperability between different localisation applications. The Localisation Industry Standards Association (LISA – www.lisa.org) has developed various localisation standards:

- Translation Memory Exchange (TMX) for exchanging TM database content. Many TM tool providers have implemented support for TMX in their products.
- Term Base eXchange (TBX): XML Terminology Exchange Standard. An XML linking standard, called Term Link, is also being investigated.
- Segmentation Rules eXchange (SRX), for exchanging the rule by which content is originally segmented. There has been very little support to date for SRX because segmentation is the main component that distinguished TM tools. Segmentation has direct consequences for the level of reuse of a TM. A TM's value is significantly reduced without the segmentation rules that were used to build it.
- Global information management Metrics eXchange (GMX): A partially populated family of standards of globalization and localization-related metrics

The Organization for the Advancement of Structured Information Standards (OASIS – www.oasis-open.org), which produces e-business standards has had a number of initiatives:

- XML Localisation Interchange File Format (XLIFF): XLIFF is the most common open standard for the exchange of localisable con-

tent and localisation process information between tools in a workflow. Many tool providers have implemented support for XLIFF in their products.
- Trans-WS for automating the translation and localization process as a Web service. There has not been much adoption of this standard. Work on the development and maintenance of the standard seems to be at a stand-still.
- Open Architecture for XML Authoring and Localization: A recently started group looking at linking many existing localisation standards

The W3C, which develops many web standards, has an Internationalisation Activity (www.w3.org/International) working on enabling the use Web technologies with different languages, scripts, and cultures. Specific standardisation includes the Internationalisation Tag Set to support internationalisation of XML Schema/DTDs.

To date, therefore, standard localisation processes and workflows addressing common interoperability issues have not yet been widely adopted. Outside of proprietary scenarios, digital publishers and service providers cannot integrate their processes and technologies and cannot provide independent performance measures. This implies lost business opportunities for many and missed opportunities for significant performance improvement for most of the stakeholders. We now examine how web services may help improve this situation.

3 Service Oriented Localization Integration

The Centre for Next Generation Localisation [cngl] is developing a number of systems in order to investigate the issues that arise in integrating centralized workflows with community-based value creation. It aims to make full use of Service-Oriented Architecture [erl]. This advocates software integration through well defined functional interfaces that can be invoked remotely, typically using the Web's HTTP protocol with input and output parameters encoded in XML. The W3C have standardized an XML format, The Web Service Description Language (WSDL), for describing and exchanging such service definitions. Web services can be composed into more complicated applications using explicit control and data flow models that can be directly executed by workflow engines. This allows new workflow applications to be defined declaratively and immediately executed, thus greatly reducing the integration costs of developing new workflows and increasing the flexibility to modify existing ones. Such web-service based service composition is known as Web Service Orchestration. OASIS has standardized web service orchestration language called the Business Process Execution Language (BPEL), which has resulted in the development of several commercial execution platform and BPEL workflow definition tools, which support workflow definition through drag-and drop interfaces. In CNGL, web services and web service orchestration are used for integrating components and operating workflows between potential partners in the commercial localization value chain. This provides a high degree of flexibility in integrating the different language technologies and localization products into different workflow configurations for the project, while avoiding reliance on any single proprietary platform. As an initial exploration of this space a system integration trial was undertaken. The use of BPEL for integrating NLP software has previously been used in the LanguageGrid project, but is a purely in support of academic research integration. Our work aimed flexibility instantiate commercial localisation workflow using NLP software wrapped in services that are orchestrated using BPEL, while, as indicated in Figure 1, still integrating with commercial localisation workflow tools. This exploration also included extending the human element of the localisation workflow by soliciting translations from a body of volunteer translators. This is seen as more appropriate if the required translation is not time constrained and it often forms part of a customer relationship strategy. Quality management may require involvement of volunteer post-editors, and incomplete or poor translations may ultimately still need to be referred to professional translators.

Thus our workflows can be configured to operate in parallel to provide alternative translations. In the professional localization workflow, after the MT stage, the candidate translation would be returned to the SDL Worldserver platform via which professional translators and post-editors are able to complete the task. In the crowd-sourcing variation, this manual step is instead performed by passing the job to a similar application implemented as a plug-in to the Drupal collaborative content management system.

Our implementation uses the XLIFF format as a standard for encapsulating the various transformations that happen to a resource as it passes through the localisation process. It should be noted, however, that support for XLIFF is partial at best in most localisation tools. Where the standard is supported, there are often different, specific flavours used, and embedded elements within the XLIFF can be lost as the resource passes through various stages in the process. Another problem with incorporating current tools in our service-oriented framework is that some of them, such as IBM's UIMA, are designed to function in a batch mode – which does not map cleanly to services. Nevertheless, despite a range of practical problems, it was in general possible to engineer service front-ends for most of these tools so that they can be integrated into a composable service infrastructure. In the following section we proceed to detail the design of the generic web services we defined for this system and discuss the option undertaken in their implementation.

3.1 Web Service Definitions

The OASIS TWS working group remains the only real attempt to define web-services to support the localization process. However, TWS has a limited scope. Rather than aiming to support the dynamic composition of language services into flexible localization workflows, it concentrates on supporting the negotiation of "jobs" between service providers. It is primarily intended to support the efficient out-sourcing of localization and translation jobs and it does not address the composition of language-services to form automated workflows.

Therefore, in order to deploy web-services to support such composition, there is little standardisation to rely on. Thus, a first step in addressing the problem is to design a set of web-services and their interfaces suitable for the task. In designing these services, it is worthwhile to recall the general goals of service-oriented architectures; the services should be designed to be as flexible and general as possible and they should neither be tightly coupled to one another, nor to the overall system which they are part of. Furthermore, in keeping with the general trends in service designs [foster], variability in service behavior should generally be supported through the passed data-structures rather than through different function signatures.

Bearing these design goals in mind, we can begin to analyse the basic requirements of localisation with a view to translating these requirements into concrete service definitions. However, in order to further simplify this task, we adopt certain assumptions about the data-formats that will be deployed. Firstly, we assume that UTF-8 is the universal character encoding scheme in use across our services. Secondly, we assume that XLIFF is employed as the standard format for exchanging localization data between different parts of the localisation process.

XLIFF is primarily focused on describing a resource in terms of source segments and target segments. Essentially, it assumes the following model: a localization job can be divided up into a set of translatable resources. Each of these resources is represented as an XLIFF file. Each resource can be further sub-divided into a sequence of translatable segments (which may be defined by an SRX configuration). Each of these source segments can be associated with a number of target segments, which represent the source segment translated into a target language. Finally, XLIFF also supports the association of various pieces of meta-data with each resource or with the various elements into which the resource is sub-divided.

This simple basic structure allows us to define a very simple set of general web-services, each of which serves to transform the XLIFF in some way. These three basic classes of services transform the XLIFF inputs in the following ways:

1. Addition of target segments.
2. Sorting of target candidates
3. Addition of meta-data.

Thus, we adopt these service-types as the set of basic, general service interfaces that our services will implement. They allow us to apply a wide range of useful language-technology processes to localization content through an extremely simple set of service interfaces. To give some examples of how concrete services map onto these basic interfaces:

- A machine translation service is a manifestation of type 1. It adds translations, as target segments, for source segments in the XLIFF file

- A translation memory leveraging service is, similarly, implemented as a service of type 1. It can be considered as a special case of a translation service.
- Our basic service-design supports the application of multiple TM and MT services to each XLIFF file, potentially producing multiple translation candidates for each source segment. There are various situations where there is a need to order these candidates – for example to choose which one will actually be used in the final translation, or to present a sorted list to a human user to allow them to most conveniently select the candidate that is most likely to be selected by them. These services can be implemented using the common type 2 interface.
- A wide range of text analytics service can be implemented as services of type 3. For example, domain identification, language identification and various tagging services are all instantiations of this type.

Although these service types are generic, in terms of the transformations that they apply to the XLIFF content, they may be very different in terms of their management and configuration. Thus, it is neither possible nor desirable to devise generic management interfaces – these interfaces need to be tailored to the particular requirements of each specific service. Thus, each service really consists of two specifications – an implementation of the generic interface which allows the service to be easily integrated as a standard component into a workflow that transforms the XLIFF content, and a specific interface that defines how the service can be configured and managed. The following section provides several examples of specific services and their management interfaces.

Although XLIFF provides significant support for management of the transformation of resources as they proceed through the localisation workflow, it is not a universal solution. It is an inherently resource-oriented standard and it is thus not well suited for the aggregation of meta-data that has broader scope than that of the translatable resource. For example, in the course of a localisation workflow, we may wish to store state information relating to the user, the project, the workflow itself or various other entities that are not expressible as XLIFF resources. Therefore, a service-oriented localization workflow has a need for a service which allows the setting and retrieving of such meta-data. The following section also includes a basic outline of a service which can provide such functionality across the localization workflow.

Finally, it should be pointed out that BPEL does not provide a universal solution to the problem of constructing workflows. It is primarily designed to facilitate the orchestration of automated web-services and does not map well to human processes. This has been acknowledged in the proposed BPEL4People extension and the incorporation of better support for human tasks is also a key motivating factor for the development of the YAWL workflow specification language – a BPEL alternative [vanderaalst]. To overcome this limitation, we have designed a general purpose service which allows components to query the state of human tasks within the workflow – this allows workflows to be responsive to the progress of human tasks (e.g. by redirecting a task that is taking too long).

3.2 An MT Web Service

As part of our work within CNGL in the development of a Localisation Factory we have engineered a web service capable of leveraging translations from multiple automated translation components. The service operates by taking in an XLIFF document, iterating the segments of the document and getting a translation from each of the translation components for each segment. These translations are attached to the segment within the XLIFF and the service returns the final XLIFF document back to the client. The service can be configured to use any permutation of the automated translation components depending on the workflow in which the service finds itself operating. Some translation components may be inappropriate in a given workflow context and may be removed. The service also allows for the weighting of translations coming from different translation components so that certain translations are preferred above others.

The service implementation leverages translation from two open web based translation systems Microsoft Live Translator [mslive] and Yahoo Babelfish [babelfish]. Microsoft Live Translator can be accessed through a web service interface. Yahoo Babelfish has no web service interface so getting back translations is implemented through a screen-scraping technique on the HTML document returned.

The service also makes use of MaTrEx [matrex], a hybrid statistical/example-based machine translation system developed by our partner university Dublin City University. MaTreX makes use of the open-source Moses decoder [moses]. Translation models are created using MaTreX and are passed to the Moses decoder which performs that translation from source to target language. We took the Moses decoder and wrapped it in a web service. The web service pipes segments for translation to Moses which responds with translations. This translation model is produced based on aligned source and target corpora of content representative of the content passing through the workflow.

Finally we have taken a translation memory product LanguageExchange from Alchemy, an industrial partner within the project, and added that to the list of automated translation components available to our service. This allows any previous human translations to be leveraged during the automated translation process.

The service is engineered using Business Process Execution Language (BPEL) to orchestrate the calling of the various translation components that compose the service. BPEL allows those managing the service to easily compose a particular configuration of the service. Translation components can be easily added or removed from the service. The tool support around BPEL means that the user does not need a background in programming to develop a particular configuration of the components.

One problem we encountered implementing the MT service as a wrapper around existing components was that they are unable to handle internal markup within the segments. Segments passing through a localisation workflow are likely to contain markup to indicate particular formatting of the text. The machine translation components are only able to handle free text and the markup is not preserved during translation. Another problem encountered in using free web services over the Internet was that implementations did not encourage volume invocations, with source IP addresses requesting high volumes being blacklisted.

3.3 A Text Analytics Web Service

We have implemented a generic text-categorization service to provide text-analytic support for localization workflows. It takes an XLIFF file as input and produces an XLIFF file as output, transforming it by adding meta-data (a type 3 transform). The meta-data can be added either on a file-basis or on a segment basis, depending on the requirements of the workflow as expressed in the service's configuration. The service provides a simple and generic XLIFF transformation as part of the localization workflow, while the management interface provides flexible configurability.

The management interface is designed in order to support multiple text analytic engines, each of which can support multiple categorization schema at once. Our implementation uses two text engines, the open source TextCat package [textcat] and IBM's Fragma software [fragma]. The following operations are provided by the service:

Operation createSchema: The createSchema function creates a new categorisation schema based on a provided set of training data, which can optionally be provided by an RSS feed for ongoing training data updates.

Operation getEngines: This returns a list (encoded in XML) of the categorisation engines that are available to the Service. This allows the client to specify that a specific categorisation engine be used in subsequent requests.

Operation viewSchema: This returns a list of the categories contained within a schema (and the details of the engine that was used to create it).

Operation addData: This operation adds a piece of training data to a categorisation schema - i.e. it allows components to tell the service that a piece of text has a known category of categoryID according to the schema with schemaID.

Operation categorise: This provides a categorisation of text provided as an XLIFF segment, according to a specified schema taken form the list supported by the service.

3.4 A Crowd-sourcing Web Service

In order to allow the localization workflow to incorporate crowd-sourcing, by which we mean collaborative input from a volunteer web-based user-community, we have designed and implemented a web-service interface. This interface is designed to allow stages in the localization job to be handed off to such a community. From the point of view of the workflow, the important thing is that the localisation requirements can be adequately specified and that the status of the job can be ascertained by other elements in the workflow – allowing them to react to the progress (or lack thereof) in the task and, for example, to allow the job to be redirected to another process when it is not progressing satisfactorily.

Our service design is focused on supporting crowd-sourcing, but it is intended to extend it to offer general-purpose support for the integration of human-tasks into a BPEL workflow. It serves as a testbed and proof of concept for the development of a generic localization human task interface. The initial specification has been derived from the TWS specification [tws], but incorporates several important changes. Firstly, it is greatly simplified by removing all the quote-related functions and replacing them with the RequestJob and SubmitJob functions and combining all of the job control functions into a single updateJob function and combining the two job list functions into one.

TWS, as a standard focused on support for localization outsourcing – hence the concentration on negotiating 'quotes' between partners. Our requirements are quite different – we cannot assume that there is any price, or even any formal agreement which governs crowd-sourcing. Indeed, in general, a major problem with TWS which hindered its uptake is that it assumed a particular business model – in practice localization jobs are not so automated, nor so quick that automated price negotiation is a particularly desired feature. Such information can be incorporated into a Job Description data structure, but a generic human-task interface should not assume any particular business model – hence the significant changes between our API and that of TWS. Nevertheless, there is much clear and well-structured thinking contained in the TWS standard – how best to describe language pairs, jobs and various other commonly referenced ideas in a localization workflow. By using TWS as a base, we can take advantage of all of that work rather than designing our own data-structures from scratch. The main operation are as follows:

Operation requestJob: The JobDescription input parameter is an XML format which contains details of the job that is being requested. The returned datatype is the details of the job that is offered by the service. These are not necessarily the same. For example, the requested job might contain several language pairs, but the returned description might not contain all of these language pairs as some of those requested might not be available in the service. Generally, it can be assumed that the service will make its "best effort" to fulfill the requirements and the returned data will be as close as it can get to the requirements submitted.

Operation submitJob: This operation works exactly as the one above, except for the fact that it submits the job to the service with the particular JobDescription required and receives back the JobDescription that will actually be carried out.

Operation retrieveJobList: This accepts a JobDescription input parameter, an XML format which contains a 'filter' on the various active jobs. The operation will return a list of all of the jobs which match that specified in the JobdDescription argument.

Operation updateJob: A JobDescription input parameter is an XML format which contains a description of the various changes to the job that are being requested. The function will return a description which details the new, updated state of the job (note that the service does not have to follow all the requested changes and might ignore them).

Operation retrieveJob: A JobDescription input parameter is an XML format which contains a 'filter' on the various jobs. The operation returns a URI from which the client can retrieve the localised content corresponding to the filters.

Operation associateResource: This functions associates a resource (TM / Glossary / etc) with a particular job. The returned value is the URI of the resource (which may be different than the passed ResURI). The types of resource supported will need to be decided upon.

4 Future Work: Translation Quality

The next challenge to applying these techniques to workable industrial workflows is to fully address the metrology of such workflows. The current approach does not support the instrumentation of web services to provide quality measurements. Further, such quality measures need to be provided in a way that is relevant to the quality of the workflow as a whole and the business-driven key performance indicators which it aims to support.

However, the integration of translation quality metrics across different forms of workflow and different industrial workflow components and linguistic technologies has been widely identified as requiring considerable further investigation. Even the most basic metric used in commercial workflow, the word count against which translation effort is estimated, is calculated differently by different workflow systems. This particular case has already been addressed by LISA though its proposal for Global information management Metrics eXchange (GMX) [gmx].

It is hardly surprising, therefore, that closing the gap between the metrics typically used by MT system developers and what is needed to support the use of MT in commercial localization workflows is likely to be even more challenging. For example, metrics such as BLEU [bleu] are well-understood by MT developers used to participating in large-scale open MT evaluations such as NIST; a BLEU score of 0.8 (say) means either that one's MT system is extremely good, or that the task is quite simple, or both, or even that there are a large number of reference translations against which the system output is being compared. On the other hand, a score of 0.2 means that the quality is poor, that there is probably only one reference translation against which candidate translations are being evaluated, or that the task is a very complex one.

However, neither score means anything (much) to a potential user. In the localization industry, Translation Memory is much more widely used, and there users and vendors use a different metric, namely fuzzy match score, i.e. how closely a previously translated source sentence matches the current input string. Users typically 'know' that a score of around 70% fuzzy match is useful, whereas for a lower scored sentence it is likely to be quicker to translate this from scratch.

One of our research goals in the CNGL is to bring these two communities closer together by developing a translation quality metric that speaks to both sets of people, developers and users. One step in the right direction might be the Translation Edit Rate metric [ter], which measures the number of editing commands (deletions, substitutions, and insertions) that need to be carried out in order to transform the MT output into the reference translation(s). This is being quite widely used in the MT community (cf. the Global Autonomous Language Exploitation (GALE) project) by MT developers, and speaks a language that users understand well. User studies will very much inform the directions that such research will take, but there are reasons to believe that the gap can be bridged.

Supposing then that such hurdles can be overcome, broadly speaking, the quality of a translation process might be dependent on multiple factors, each of which could be measured both intrinsically and extrinsically, including;

- Source and destination languages
- Content domain
- Diversity of vocabulary
- Repetitiveness of text
- Length and complexity of sentences
- Availability of relevant translation memories
- The cost and time incurred per translated word

Often control of quality of the translation process can be impacted most directly by the quality of the human translators and the degree of control exerted over the source text. Different levels of linguistic quality assurance may be undertaken and post-editors (who are often more experienced translators and therefore more expensive) are involved in handling incomplete or missing translations. However, even in professional translation environments, translation quality is regarded as relatively subjective and exact measurement of the quality of translation is therefore problematic.

5 Conclusion

In this paper we have discussed some the challenges faced in taking a web service integration and orchestration approach to the development of next generation localization workflows. Based on our experiences of using these approaches to integrate both existing localization products and cutting edge research prototypes in MT , TA and crowd-sourcing, new, innovative localisation workflows can be rapidly assembled. The maturity of the BPEL standard and the design of general purpose, reusable web service interfaces are key to this success.

Acknowledgments: This research is supported by the Science Foundation Ireland (Grant 07/CE/I1142) as part of the Centre for Next Generation Localisation (www.cngl.ie) at Trinity College Dublin.

References

[babelfish] Yahoo Babelfish Machine Translation http://babelfish.yahoo.com/ 6th Feb 2009

[drupal] Drupal Content Management System http://www.drupal.org 6th Feb 2009

[bleu] Kishore Papineni, Salim Roukos, Todd Ward and Wei-Jing Zhu. 2002. In 40th Annual Meeting of the Association for Computational Linguistics, Philadelphia, PA., pp.311—318.

[bpel] Web Services Business Process Execution Language Version 2.0, OASIS Standard, 11 April 2007, Downloaded from http://docs.oasis-open.org/wsbpel/2.0/OS/wsbpel-v2.0-0S.html 6th Feb 2009

[erl] Erl, Thomas, Service-oriented Architecture: Concepts, Technology, and Design. Upper Saddle River: Prentice Hall 2005

[foster] Foster, I., Parastatidis, S., Watson, P., and Mckeown, M. 2008. How do I model state?: Let me count the ways. Commun. ACM 51, 9 (Sep. 2008), 34-41.

[fragma] Alexander Troussov, Mayo Takeuchi, D.J.McCloskey, http://atroussov.com/uploads/TSD2004_LangID_word_fragments.pdf 6th Feb 2009

[gmx] Global Information Management Metrics Volume (GMX-V) 1.0 Specification Version 1.0, 26 February 2007, downloaded from http://www.xml-intl.com/docs/specification/GMX-V.html on 6th Feb 2009

[langexchange] Alchemy Language Exchange http://www.alchemysoftware.ie/products/alchemy_language_exchange.html 6th Feb 2009

[matrex] MaTrEx Machine Translation - John Tinsley, Yanjun Ma, Sylwia Ozdowska, Andy Way. http://doras.dcu.ie/559/1/Tinsleyetal_WMT08.pdf

[moses] Moses decoder http://www.statmt.org/moses/ 9th March 2009

[mslive] Microsoft Live Translator http://www.windowslivetranslator.com/ 6th Feb 2009

[ter] Matt Snover, Bonnie Dorr, Richard Schwartz, Linnea Micciulla, and John Makhoul. 2006. A Study of Translation Edit Rate with Targeted Human Annotation. In Proceedings of the 7th Conference of the Association for Machine Translation in the Americas, Cambridge, MA., pp.223—231.

[textcat] Java Text Categorisation http://textcat.sourceforge.net/ 6th Feb 2009

[tbx] Termbase eXchange Format http://www.lisa.org/Term-Base-eXchange.32.0.html 6th March 2009

[tmx] Translation Memory eXchange http://www.lisa.org/Translation-Memory-e.34.0.html 6th March 2009

[tws] Translation Web Services Specification: http://www.oasis-open.org/committees/download.php/24350/trans-ws-spec-1.0.3.html

[vanderaalst] Van Der Aalst, W.M.P. Ter Hofstede, A.H.M. "YAWL: Yet another workflow language" Information Systems, Volume 30, Issue 4, June 2005, Pages 245-275

[xliff] XML Localisation Interchange File Format http://docs.oasis-open.org/xliff/v1.2/os/xliff-core.html 6th March 2009

Distributed Parse Mining

Scott A. Waterman, PhD
Microsoft Live Search/Powerset
475 Brannan St.
San Francisco, USA
waterman@acm.org

Abstract

We describe the design and implementation of a system for data exploration over dependency parses and derived semantic representations in a large-scale NLP-based search system at `powerset.com`. Because of the distributed nature of the document repository and the processing infrastructure, and also the complex representations of the corpus data, standard text analysis tools such as `grep` or `awk` or language modeling toolkits are not applicable. This paper explores the challenges of extracting statistical information and of building language models in such a distributed NLP environment, and introduces a corpus analysis system, *Oceanography*, that simplifies the writing of analysis code and transparently takes advantage of existing distributed processing infrastructure.

1 Introduction

In computational linguistics we deal with large corpora and vast amounts of data from which we would like to extract useful information. The size of the text resources, derived linguistic analyses, and the complexity of their representations is often a stumbling block on the way to understanding the statistical and linguistic behavior within the corpus. Simple software tools suffice for small or simple analysis problems, or for building models of easily represented relations. However, as the size of data, the intricacy of relations to be analyzed, and the complexity of the representation grow, so too does the technical difficulty of conducting the analysis.

Software is our given means of escape from this escalation of complexity. However, as "computational linguists," we often find ourselves spending more time and attention building software to perform the required *computations* than we do on understanding the linguistics.

Even once a suitable set of NLP tools (e.g. taggers, chunkers, parsers, etc.) has been chosen, analysis software, in the CL world, often consists of "throw away" scripts. Small, *ad hoc* programs are often the norm, often with no assurance (via strict design or testing) of correctness or completeness.

1.1 Oceanography

Our goal is to ensure that analysis is not so problematic. Powerset is a group within the Microsoft Live Search team focused on using semantic NLP to improve web search. We face many problems with the scale and integration of our NLP components, and are approaching solving them by applying sound software design and abstraction principles to corpus processing. By generalizing tools to fit the processing environment, and the nature of the problems at hand, we enable flexible processing which scales with the size of the platform and the data.

The *Oceanography* software environment is designed to address two important needs in large corpus analysis. The first is to simplify the actual programming of analysis code to reduce development time and increase reliability, and the second is to use the available distributed computing resources to reduce running time and provide for rapid testing and experimental turnaraound.

Proceedings of the NAACL HLT Workshop on Software Engineering, Testing, and Quality Assurance for Natural Language Processing, pages 56–64,
Boulder, Colorado, June 2009.

1.2 Linguistic and Diagnostic data analysis

There are two separate kinds of analysis we want to support over this processed corpus. The first is linguistic modeling. In order to achieve the best semantic interpretation of each source document, we seek to understand the linguistic behavior within the corpus. Probabilistic parsing, entity extraction, sense disambiguation, and argument role assignment are all informed by structured, statistical models of word behavior within the corpus. Some models can be built from simple tokenized text, while other models need to incorporate parse dependencies or real-word knowledge of entities. Some of these tasks are exploratory and underspecified (e.g. selectional restrictions), while others, such as name tagging, have a well-developed literature and a number of almost standard methodologies.

The second kind of analysis is aimed at characterizing and improving system behavior. For example, distributions of POS-tags or preposition attachments can serve as regression indicators for parser performance. In order to perform error analysis, we need to selectively sample various types of label assignments or parse structures. So summarization and sampling from the various intermediate NL analyses are very important processes to support.

2 Generalizing Text Mining

We have found that most of these analysis and data modeling tasks share certain higher order steps that allow us to generalize them all into a single programming framework. All involve identifying some phenomena in one of the NLP outputs, representing it in some characteristic form, and then summing or comparing distributions. These general steps apply to many corpus tasks, including building n-gram data, learning sentence breaks, identifying selectional preferences, or building role mappings for verb nominalizations.

The Oceanography system generalizes these steps into a declarative language for stating the selection of data, and the form of output, in a way that avoids repetitive and error prone boilerplate code for file traversal, regular expression matching, and statistics programming. By matching a declarative syntax to the general analysis steps, these common functions can be relegated to library code, or wrapped into the executable in the compilation step. The less time spent in describing a task, or in coding and debugging the implementation, the more time and attention can be spent in understanding the results and modeling the linguistic processes that underly the data.

This sort of abstraction away from the details of file representation, storage architecture, and processing model fits a general trend toward data mining, or *text mining* (Feldman and Dagan, 1995). In data mining or KDD systems (Fayyad et al., 1996), the goal is to separate the tasks of creative analysis and theorizing from the mundane aspects of traversing the data collection and computing statistics. These are much the same goals emphasized by Tukey (1977) – exploration of the data and interactions in order to understand which hypotheses, and which models of interaction, would be fruitful to explore. For our needs in analyzing collections of text, parses, and semantic representations, we have achieved a very practical step toward these goals.

2.1 Matching process to conception

We have found four steps that map very closely to our conception of the data analysis problem, which at the same time are easily translated to implementations that can be run on both small local data sets and on very large distributed corpora.

1. **Pattern matching** – find the interesting phenomena among the mass of data, by declaring a set of desired properties to be met. In Oceanography, these are matched per-sentence.

2. **Transformation** – rewrite the raw occurrence data to identify the interesting part, and isolate it from the background

3. **Aggregation** – group together instances of the same kind

4. **Statistics** – compute statistics for counts, relative frequency, conditional distributions, distributional comparisons, etc.

In the following sections we describe the nature of each step in more detail, map these steps to a declarative data analysis language, give some motivating examples, and describe how these steps are typically accomplished in an exploratory setting for NLP investigations.

Later, in section 4, we describe how the steps are mapped to processing operations within the NLP pipeline architecture. Following that, we give examples of how this framework maps to specific problems, of both the exploratory and the diagnostic type.

2.2 Pattern Matching

The first step is to identify the specific phenomena of interest within the source data. If the data is a complex structure, it is helpful to express the patterns in a logical representation of the structure, rather than matching the representation directly.

Pattern matching in Oceanography for dependency parse structures is handled using a domain specific language (DSL) built explicitly for pattern-based manipulation of parse trees and semantic representations generated by the XLE linguistic components (Crouch et al., 2006). This *Transfer* language (Crouch, 2006) is normally used in the regular linguistic processing pipeline to incrementally rewrite LFG dependency parses into a role-labeled semantic representations (*semreps*) of entities, events, and relations in the text. Transfer matches pattern rules to a current set of parse dependencies or semantic facts, and writes alternate expressions derived from the matched components. Variables in these expressions are bound via Prolog-style unification (Huet, 1975).

For example, in figure 1, the first expression `word(···)` will match word forms in a parse that are `'verb'`s, and bind `%VerbSk` variable to a unique occurrence id and `%VerbWord` to the verb lemma. The second pattern finds the node in the dependency graph that fills the `ob` (object) role for that verb, and extracts its lemmas. (The `%%`'s are placeholder variables in the pattern, needed to match the arity of the expression.) Below, in the same figure, is a representation of the verb and object from a parse of the phrase "determined the structure". On matching these facts, the `VerbWord` and `ObjLemma` variables would be bound to the strings `determine` and `structure`.

In a simpler environment, with more basic textual representations, this pattern matching step would be written with regular expressions, for example using the familiar `grep` command. The balance provided by `grep` between the simplicity of its operational model (a transform from stdin to stdout) and the expressiveness of the regular expressions allows `grep` to be a workhorse for data analysis over text.

However, except for simple cases such as word cooccurrence models, the typical need in deep linguistic analysis is not well served by regular expressions over strings. Anyone in the NLP field who has written regular expressions to match, say, part-of-speech labeled text knows the difficulties of having a pattern language which differs from the logical structures being matched. Another typical solution is to write a short program in a scripting language (e.g. perl, python, SNOBOL) which combines regular expressions to provide a simple structure parser. Tgrep (Pito, 1993) is a one such program which extends this regular expression notion to patterns over trees, and can output subtrees matching those expressions, but only provided they are represented as text in the LDC TreeBank format.

2.3 Transformation

Once the items of the pattern have been identified in their original context, it is often necessary to isolate them from that context, and remove the extraneous, irrelevant information. For instance, if one is doing a simple word count, the tokenized words of text must be separated from any annotation and counted independently. For more complicated tasks, such as finding a verb's distribution of occurrence with direct objects, the verb and object need to be isolated from the remainder of the parse tree, perhaps as the simple tuple *(verb, object)*, or in a more complex structure, with additional dependent information.

In our case, we express the transformed output of each pattern match with an expression built from the unification variables bound to the match. In figure 2, we construct a `vo_pair` of *(verb, object)*. This new construct is simply added to the collection of facts and representations already present. All other preexisting facts in the NL analysis of the sentence also remain in context, potentially available for aggregation and counting.

```
==> vo_pair(%VerbWord, %ObjLemma).
```

Figure 2: Transforming the matched pattern

```
word(%VerbSk, %VerbWord, verb, verb, %%, %%, %%, %% ),
in_context(%%, role(hier(ob, %%), %VerbSk, %ObjLemma:%%))
```

```
word(determine:n(41,3),determine,verb,verb, ....)
in_context(t,role(hier(ob,[[ob,root],..]),
        determine:n(82,3),structure:n(91,3))))
```

Figure 1: Pattern matching using Transfer

In shallower text mining, this might be accomplished using regex matching in a perl program. Another common approach is to use command-line text tools such as `awk` or `sed`. `Awk` (Aho et al., 1977) is designed especially for text mining, but is limited to plain text files, on single machines, and doesn't extend easily to structured graph representations or distributed processing. (But see, e.g. Sawzall (Pike et al., 2005) for a scalable awk-like language.)

2.4 Aggregation

The aggregation step collects the extracted instances and groups them by type and by key. Rather than have the matched, transformed results simply dumped out in some enormous file or database in their order of occurrence in the data set (as one would get e.g. from `grep`), it is quite useful even in the simplest of cases to aggregate all similar output items. This condenses the mass of data selected, and allows one to see the extent and diversity of the items that are found by the patterns. This simple counting is often enough for diagnostic tasks, and sometimes for exploratory tasks when a statistical judgement is not yet desired. The aggregation key might be, for various kinds of extraction: the head noun of an NN-compound, or the error type for parse errors, or the controlling verb of a relative clause.

In Oceanography, we require a declaration of the data that will be aggregated, in order to separate it from the remainder which will be discarded. These declarations take the form of familiar static type declarations, in the style of C++ or Java. Figure 3 shows the simple declaration for our `vo_pair` type, where both fields are declared as strings. These named fields also provide a handle to refer to structure members in later statements.

In the command line text world, aggregation might be accomplished by using the unix pipeline command `sort | uniq -c`, to organize the output by the appropriate key. If using a small program to do this kind of analysis, one would use a dictionary or hash-table and sorting routines to organize the data before output.

```
vo_pair :: {
    verb::String, object::String }
```

Figure 3: Declaring aggregation types

2.5 Statistics

With the matched and extracted data, one can build up a statistical picture of the data and its interrelations. In our practice, and in the computational NLP literature, we have found a few fundamental statistical operations that are frequently used to make sense of the corpus data. Primary among these are simple class counts: the number of occurrences of a given phenomena. For instance, the count of part-of-speech tags, or of head nouns with adjective modifiers, or the counts of *(verb,object)* pairs. These counts can be computed easily by summing the occurrences in the aggregated groups.

Other statistics are more complicated, requiring combinations of the simple counts and sums — normalizing distributions by the total occurrence counts, for instance, as in the conditional occurrence of a part-of-speech label relative to the frequency of the token. Estimation of log-likelihood ratios or Pearson's Chi-square test for pairwise correlation also falls in this category. These kinds of computations are used heavily for building classifiers and for diagnostic purposes.

Higher order functions of the counts are also interesting, in which various distributions compared. These include computing KL distance between conditional distributions for similarity measurements, clustering over similarity, and building predictive or classification models for model corpus behavior.

3 Data Parallel Document Processing at Powerset

To simplify the processing of large web document collections, and flexibly include new processing modules, we have built a single consistent processing architecture for the natural language document pipeline, which allows us to process millions of documents and handle terabytes of analysis data effectively. *Coral* is the name of the distributed, document-parallel NLP pipeline at Powerset. Coral provides both a process and a data management framework in order to smoothly execute the multi-step linguistic analysis of all content indexed for Powerset's search.

Coral controls a multi-step pipeline for deep linguistic processing of documents indexed for search. A partial list of the steps every web document undergoes includes: HTML destructuring, sentence breaking, name tagging, parsing, semantic interpretation, anaphora resolution, and indexing. The pipeline is similar to the UIMA (Ferrucci and Lally, 2004) architecture in that each step adds intermediate data — tagged spans, dependency trees, coreferent expressions — that can be used in subsequent steps. Each step adds a different kind of data to the set, with its own labels and meanings. The output of all these steps is a daunting amount of information, all of which is valuable for understanding the linguistic relations within the text, and also the behavior and effectiveness of the NLP pipeline.

Documents are processed in a data-parallel fashion. Multiple documents are processed independently, across multiple processes on multiple compute nodes within a clustered environment. The document processing model is sequential, with multiple steps run in a fixed sequence for each document in the index. All processing for a single document is typically performed on a single compute node. The steps of the pipeline communicate through intermediate data writen to the local filesystem in between steps, where each step is free to consume data produced earlier. Output from the stages is checkpointed to backing storage at various points along the way, and the final index fragments are merged at the end.

This kind of data-parallel process lends itself well to a map/reduce programming infrastructure (Dean and Ghemawat, 2004). Map/reduce divides processing into two classes: data-parallel 'map' operations, and commutative 'reduce' operations, in which all map output aggregated under a particular key is processed together. In map/reduce terms, the entire linguistic processing runs as a sequence of 'map' steps (there is no inter-document communication), with a final 'reduce' step to collect index fragments and construct a unified search index. Coral uses the open-source hadoop implementation of map/reduce (Cutting,) as the central task control and distribution mechanism for assigning NLP pipeline jobs to documents in the input data, and it has full control of the map/reduce processing layer.

3.1 Difficulties for data mining in Coral

All of the intermediate processing output of the pipeline, the name tags, parses, semantic representations, etc., are are retained by this complex process. Unfortunately, they are retained in an unfriendly format: small document-addressed chunks scattered across a large distributed filesystem, on hundreds of machines. There is no operational way to collect these chunks in any single file, or to traverse them efficiently from any single point. Traditional scripting techniques, even if scalable to the terabytes of data, are not applicable to the distributed organization of the underlying data.

3.2 Re-using processing infrastructure for mining

However, we can re-use the same Coral process and data management for the problems of data analysis. The breakdown of parse-mining steps presented earlier, in addition to providing a coherent model for data analysis, also maps very cleanly to the distributed map/reduce computational model. By translating the four steps of any analysis into corresponding map/reduce operations across the linguistic pipeline data, we can efficiently translate the corpus analytics to an arbitrarily large data setting. Further, because we can rely on the Coral process and data management infrastructure to handle the data movement and traversal, we allow the researcher or language engineer to concentrate on specifying the patterns and relations to be investigated, rather than burdening them with complex yet necessary details.

4 Oceanography - a compiled data mining language

Oceanography has a compiler that transforms short analysis programs into multiple map/reduce steps that will operate over the corpus of text and deep linguistic analyses. These multiple sub-operations are then farmed out through the distributed cluster environment, managed by the Coral job controller. The data flow and dependencies between these jobs are compiled to a Coral-specific job control language.

An oceanography program (cf. figure 4) is a single-file description of the data analysis task. It contains specifications for each of the four operations: pattern matching, transformation, aggregation, and statistics. The program style is declarative – there are no instructions for iterating over files, summing distributions, or parsing the dependency graph representations.

We find that this matches our intuitions and conception of the parse mining task. A statement of the end-product of the analysis is natural: e.g. find the conditional distribution of object head nouns for verbs, or symbolically $p(obj|verb)$. The style of the oceanography program matches this well, where the statistics statement such as

```
dist triple.object cond on triple.verb
```

states the desired output, and the preceding pattern match and type declarations serve as definitions to specify precisely what is meant by the variable names.

In the following sections, we will follow the steps of the Oceanography program in the listing in figure 4. The example analysis presented is a simple one – to find all verbs with both subject and object roles, i.e. triples of *(subject, object, verb)*, and report some counts and relative frequencies of verbs, subjects, and objects.

4.1 Step 1: Pattern Matching

The pattern matching rules are similar to those presented above in sec. 2.2. The first line matches a verb term, and the next two lines require the presence of terms in both the subject (`role(hier(sb, %%))`) and object `role(hier(ob, %%))` roles. Following the explicit pattern expression, we add negative checks to ensure that neither the subject or object are PRO elements, which have no surface form.

4.2 Transformation

The transformation expressed in figure 4 is almost trivial. We capture the verb-subject-object triple in a simple three place predicate. Recall that the values of the triple:

```
(%VerbWord, %SubjLemma, %ObjLemma)
```

are bound by unification to the terms matched in the pattern, above.

Although we have only one pattern and one matching transformation in this example, we are not in general limited in the number of patterns or output expressions we might use. Multiple transforms, from multiple patterns, can be used.

During compilation, these Transfer rules are compiled into a binary object module, then distributed at runtime to the compute nodes where they will be executed in the proper sequence by the Coral job controller. Output from the transformation step, and between all the steps, is encoded as a set of hierarchically structured objects using JSON (Crockford, 2006). Because JSON provides a simple structural encoding with named fields, and many programming environments can handle the JSON format, it provides a flexible and self-describing interchange format between steps in the Oceanography runtime.

4.3 Aggregation

The third section of the Oceanography program declares the types of objects to be aggregated following the transform step. The type declarations in this section serve two purposes. First, they specify exactly what types of data from the matching/transformation phase should be carried forward. Recall that all of the source data is available for processing, but we are likely only interested in a small portion of it. Secondly, the declarations serve as type hints to the compiler so that operations and data storage are performed correctly in the later phases (e.g. adding strings vs. integers).

4.4 Statistics

The simplest statistic we can compute is the count of a type that has been aggregated. For example,

```
## Step 1: pattern matching
rules {
    word(%VerbSk, %VerbWord, verb, verb, %%Pos, %%SentNum, %%Context, %%LexicalInfo ),
    in_context(%%, role(hier(sb, %%), %VerbSk, %SubjLemma:%%)),
    in_context(%%, role(hier(ob, %%), %VerbSk, %ObjLemma:%%)),
    { \+memberchk( %SubjLemma, [group_object, null_pro, agent_pro]),
      \+memberchk( %ObjLemma, [group_object, null_pro, agent_pro])  }
## Step 2: Transformation
    ==> triple(%VerbWord, %SubjLemma, %ObjLemma).
}
## Step 3: Aggregation
triple :: {
    verb :: String,
    subject :: String,
    object :: String
}
## Step 4: Statistics
count triple
count triple.verb
count triple.verb, triple.subject
dist triple.object cond on triple.verb
```

Figure 4: A complete Oceanography program

```
count triple.verb
```

will result in occurrence counts of each verb seen in the parses. We can combine primitive types into tuples, in order to count n-grams (which are not necessarily adjacent), e.g.

```
count triple.verb, triple.subject
```

to give occurrence counts for all (verb,subject) pairs.

The `dist X cond on Y` statement is used to produce the conditional distribution $p(x|y)$. The map/reduce framework collates all occurrences with a given value y_i to a single reduce function, which sums the conditional counts of x, and normalizes by the total.

Other statistics require multiple map/reduce operations. Computing the probability for the verb unigrams requires knowing the total number of occurrences, which, in this kind of data-parallel processing architecture, is not available until the output of all occurrence counts is known. So, a `prob triple.verb` statistic must implicitly compute `count triple.verb`, sum all occurrences, and normalize across the set. For a good type-driven analysis of information flow during various stages of a map/reduce computations, see Lämmel (2008).

4.5 Output

Output is given two forms. For ease of interpretations, human-readable tab delimited files are written, in which each record is preceded by the type, as given in the argument to the statistics declaration. To simplify later offline computation, the record can also be written out in a JSON encoded structure with named fields corresponding to the type.

5 Development and testing in Oceanography

Rapid turnaround and testing in exploratory corpus analytics is essential to understanding the nature of the data, and the performance and behavior of one's program. Because the tools on which Oceanography is built are modular, we can compile an analysis program for a local, single machine target as easily as we can for a cluster of arbitrarily many compute nodes. The resulting compiled programs differ somewhat in the ways they traverse the data, and in the control structures for the Coral processing steps. However, it was an important design requirement that we could compile and test using small data on a single machine as easily as on a muti-terabyte corpus on a distributed cluster.

The same source program is compiled for either single machine or cluster execution. The user must specify a different type of store location for input and output data, depending on environment. Compilation is done using a command line program, which takes as input the Oceanography program, and produces a set of executable outputs, corresponding to the tasks in the map/reduce process. These can also be run immediately in the single machine setting, with results going to stdout.

5.1 Some sample tasks

Although these tools have been available at Powerset only a few months, we have already used them to great advantage in diagnostic and linguistic analysis tasks. Diagnostically, it is important to understand the failure modes of the various linguistic pipeline components. For instance, the morphological analysis component of the XLE parser will on occasion encounter tokens it cannot analyze. Hand-examining a few hundred parses (which starts to exceed the mental fatigue threshold), one can find numerous examples. But one has no idea of the relative frequency of any given type of error, or their combined effect on the parse output. Oceanography enables a very simple single pattern match rule to be used to find the frequency distribution of unknown tokens over 100M sentences as easily as 100, and the grammar engineers can use this information to prioritize their effort. Other diagnostics on the parse, such as the frequency of certain rare grammatical constructs (e.g. reduced relatives), or the prevalence of unparseable fragments, or relative frequencies of transitive v. intransitive use, are immensely important for understanding the nature of the corpus and the behavior of the parser.

The S-V-O triples used as an example also have practical import. By identifying the most common verb expressions, we can, just as in a keyword stop list, eliminate or downweight some of the less meaningful relations in our semantic index. For example, in the Wikipedia corpus, one of the most common S-V-O triples comes from the phrase "this article needs references."

We are also beginning a series of lexical semantic studies, looking at selectional preferences and their dependence on surface form. Correspondence between prepositional adjunct roles and other surface realizations is also an active area. Additionally, Oceanography is being used to analyze feature data from the parses in order to experiment with an unsupervised word sense disambiguation project.

6 Conclusion

We have presented a methodology for understanding a certain class of linguistic data analysis problems, which identifies the steps of pattern matching, data transformation, aggregation, and statistics. We have also presented a programming system, Oceanography, which by following this breakdown simplifies the programming of these tasks while at the same time enabling us to take advantage of existing large scale distributed processing infrastructure.

Acknowledgments

I would like to thank Jim Firby, creator of the Coral document processing pipeline at Powerset, and Dick Crouch, creator of the XLE Transfer system, for their foundational work which makes these present developments possible.

References

Alfred V. Aho, Peter J. Weinberger, and Brian W. Kernighan. 1977. awk.

D. Crockford. 2006. The application/json Media Type for JavaScript Object Notation (JSON). RFC 4627 (Informational), July.

Richard S. Crouch, Mary Dalrymple, Ronald M. Kaplan, Tracy Holloway King, John Maxwell, and P. Newman. 2006. XLE documentation.

Richard S. Crouch. 2006. Packed rewriting for mapping text to semantics and KR.

Doug Cutting. Apache Hadoop Project. http://hadoop.apache.org/.

Jeffrey Dean and Sanjay Ghemawat. 2004. MapReduce: simplified data processing on large clusters. In *OSDI'04: Proceedings of the 6th conference on Symposium on Opearting Systems Design & Implementation*, Berkeley, CA, USA. USENIX Association.

Usama M. Fayyad, David Haussler, and Paul E. Stolorz. 1996. KDD for Science Data Analysis: Issues and Examples. In *KDD*, pages 50–56.

Ronen Feldman and Ido Dagan. 1995. Knowledge Discovery in Textual Databases (KDT). In *KDD*, pages 112–117.

David Ferrucci and Adam Lally. 2004. UIMA: an architectural approach to unstructured information processing in the corporate research environment. *Nat. Lang. Eng.*, 10(3-4):327–348.

Grard P. Huet. 1975. A unification algorithm for typed lambda-calculus. *Theor. Comput. Sci*, 1:27.

Ralf Lämmel. 2008. Google's MapReduce programming model - Revisited. *Sci. Comput. Program.*, 70(1):1–30.

Rob Pike, Sean Dorward, Robert Griesemer, and Sean Quinlan. 2005. Interpreting the data: Parallel analysis with Sawzall. *Scientific Programming*, 13(4):277–298.

Richard Pito. 1993. Tgrep.

John Wilder Tukey. 1977. *Exploratory Data Analysis*. Addison-Wesley, New York.

Modular resource development and diagnostic evaluation framework for fast NLP system improvement

Gaël de Chalendar, Damien Nouvel
CEA, LIST, Multilingual Multimedia Knowledge Engineering Laboratory,
F-92265 Fontenay-aux-Roses, France.
{Gael.de-Chalendar,Damien.Nouvel}@cea.fr

Abstract

Natural Language Processing systems are large-scale softwares, whose development involves many man-years of work, in terms of both coding and resource development. Given a dictionary of 110k lemmas, a few hundred syntactic analysis rules, 20k ngrams matrices and other resources, what will be the impact on a syntactic analyzer of adding a new possible category to a given verb? What will be the consequences of a new syntactic rules addition? Any modification may imply, besides what was expected, unforeseeable side-effects and the complexity of the system makes it difficult to guess the overall impact of even small changes. We present here a framework designed to effectively and iteratively improve the accuracy of our linguistic analyzer LIMA by iterative refinements of its linguistic resources. These improvements are continuously assessed by evaluating the analyzer performance against a reference corpus. Our first results show that this framework is really helpful towards this goal.

1 Introduction

1.1 The evaluation framework

In Natural Language Processing (NLP), robustness and reliability of linguistic analyzers becomes an everyday more addressed issue, given the increasing size of resources and the amount of code implied by the implementation of such systems. Beyond choosing a sound technology, one must now have efficients and user-friendly tools around the system itself, for evaluating its accuracy. As shown by (Chatzichrisafis et al., 2008), where developers receive daily reports of system's performance for improving their system, systematic evaluation with regression testing has shown to be gainful to accelerate grammar engineering.

Evaluation campaigns, where several participants evaluate their system's performance on a specific task against other systems, are a good mean to search for directions in which a system may be able to improve its performance. Often, these evaluation campaigns also give possibility for participants to run their analyzer on test data and retrieve evaluation results. In this context, parsers authors may rely on evaluation campaigns to provide performance results, but they should also be able to continuously evaluate and improve their analyzers between evaluation campaigns. We aim at providing such a generic evaluation tool, using evaluation data to assess systems accuracy, this software will be referenced as the "Benchmarking Tool".

Approaches concerning Natural Language Processing involve everyday more and more resource data for analyzing texts. These resources have grown enough (in terms of volume and diversity), that it now becomes a challenge to manipulate them, even for experienced users. Moreover, it is needed to have non-developers being able to work on these resources: it is necessary to develop accessible tools through intuitive graphical user interfaces. Such a resource editing GUI tool represent the second part of our contribution, called the "Resource Tool".

The overall picture is to build a diagnostic framework enabling a language specialist, such as a linguist, to status, almost in real-time, how modifica-

Proceedings of the NAACL HLT Workshop on Software Engineering, Testing, and Quality Assurance for Natural Language Processing, pages 65–73,
Boulder, Colorado, June 2009.

tions impact our analyzer on as much test data as possible. For analyzers, each resource may have an effect on the final accuracy of the analysis. It is often needed to iterate over tests before understanding what resource, what part of the code needs to be improved. This is especially the case with grammar engineering, where it is difficult to predict the consequences of modifying a single rule. Ideally, our framework would allow the manipulator to slightly alter a resource, trigger an evaluation and, almost instantaneously, view results and interpret them. With this framework, we expect a large acceleration in the process of improving our analyzer.

In the remaining of this introduction, we will describe our analyzer and Passage, a collaborative project including an evaluation campaign and the production of a reference treebank for French through a voting procedure. Section 2 will describe our evaluation framework; its architecture, its two main modules and our first results using it. Section 3 describes some related works. We conclude in section 4 by describing the next steps of our work.

1.2 The LIMA linguistic analyzer

Our linguistic analyzer LIMA (LIc2m Multilingual Analyzer, (Besancon and de Chalendar, 2005)), is implemented as a pipeline of independent modules applied successively on a text. It implements a dependency grammar (Kahane, 2000) in the sense that produced analysis are exclusively represented as binary dependency relations between tokens.

The analyzer includes, among other modules, a tokenizer segmenting the text based on punctuation marks, a part of speech tagger, short and long distance dependencies extractors based on finite-state automata defined by contextualized rules. The latter rules express successions of categories, augmented with constraints (on words inflexion, existence of other dependencies, etc.). The analyzer also includes modules to find idiomatic expressions and named entities that, once recognized, are merged into a single token, thus allowing grammar rules to apply on those. Furthermore, modules may be specialized in processing language-specific phenomena, e.g. Chinese tokenization, German compounds, etc. Currently, the analyzer is able to process more or less deeply ten languages, including English, Spanish, Chinese, Arab, French and German.

1.3 The Passage Project

Our work is part of the Passage project (Clergerie et al., 2008b). The objectives of this project are twofold. Firstly, it organizes two evaluation campaigns of syntactic analyzers (around 15 participating systems) for the French language. Secondly, it aims at producing a large scale reference treebank for French by merging the output of all the participating parsers, using a Rover (Recognizer Output Voting Error Reduction) (Fiscus, 1997) approach.

Within this project, syntactic annotations are produced in a common format, rich enough to represent all necessary linguistic features and simple enough to allow participating parsers (using very different parsing approaches) to represent their analysis in this format. It is an evolution of the EASy campaign format, mixing simple non recursive chunks and dependency relations between chunks or tokens. It respects two proposed ISO specifications: MAF (ISO 24611) and SynAF (ISO 24615). The chunks and dependencies types are issued from the ISO data category registry, DCR[1], currently using the French language section names. The syntactic analysis of a corpus in the Passage format provides information about:

- Segmentation of the corpus into sentences
- Segmentation of sentences into forms
- Non-recursive typed (listed in Table 1) chunks embedding forms
- Labeled typed (listed in Table 2) dependencies that are anchored by either forms or chunks

Type	Explanation
GN	Nominal Chunk
NV	Verbal Kernel
GA	Adjectival Chunk
GR	Adverbial Chunk
GP	Prepositional Chunk
PV	Prepositional non-tensed Verbal Kernel

Table 1: Chunks types

Within the EASy project, parsers have been evaluated against a reference, which itself was a small subset of the available corpora. The reference was

[1]http://www.isocat.org

Type	Explanation
SUJ-V	Subject-verb
AUX-V	Aux-verb
COD-V	Direct objects
CPL-V	Other verb arguments/complements
MOD-V	Verb modifiers (e.g. adverbs)
COMP	Subordinate sentences
ATB-SO	Verb attribute
MOD-N	Noun modifier
MOD-A	Adjective modifier
MOD-R	Adverb modifier
MOD-P	Preposition modifier
COORD	Coordination
APPOS	Apposition
JUXT	Juxtaposition

Table 2: Dependencies types

created by human annotation of random sentences within the corpora. Thus, once this evaluation campaign had been finished, the annotated corpora reference was released for participants to test and improve their parser. Currently, we use this reference for benchmarking our analyzer.

1.4 Metrics for parsing evaluation

We are constantly recalled that evaluation metrics and methodologies evolve and are subject to intense research and innovation (Carroll et al., 2002). Discussing these metrics is not in the scope of this paper, we only need to be able to work out as many metrics as possible on the entire corpus or on any part of it. The evaluation is supposed, for each document d and for each type (of chunk or of dependency) t within all types set T, to return following counts:

- Number of items found and correct - $fc(d,t)$
- Number of items found - $f(d,t)$
- Number of items correct - $c(d,t)$

With this approach, we are able to compute common Information Retrieval (IR) metrics (Rijsbergen, 1979): precision, recall, f-measure. We also introduce a new metric that gives us indications about what types are the most lowering overall performance, called "Type error ratio":

$$\frac{f(d,t) + c(d,t) - 2.fc(d,t)}{\sum^{t \in T} f(d,t) + c(d,t) - 2.fc(d,t)} \qquad (1)$$

This metric counts the number of errors and misses for a given type reported to the total number of errors and misses. It allows us to quantify how much an improvement on a given type will improve the overall score. In our case, scores are computed for chunks on the one hand, and for dependencies on the other hand. For instance, we have notices that GN errors represent 34.6% of the chunks errors, whereas PV only represent 2.2%: we are thus much more interested in improving detection of GN than PV regarding current evaluation campaign.

2 The evaluation framework

2.1 Architecture

We need our framework to be portable and to be implemented using an agile approach: each new version should be fully functional while adding some more features. It also must be user-friendly, allowing to easily add eye-candy features. Consequently, we have chosen to implement these tools in C++, using the Qt 4.5 library[2]. This library satisfies our requirements and will allow to rely on stable and open source (LGPL) tools, making it feasible for us to possibly deliver our framework as a free software.

This approach allows us to quickly deliver working software while continuously testing and developing it. Iterations of this process are still occurring but the current version, with its core functions, already succeeded in running benchmarks and in beginning the improvement of our linguistic resources while regularly delivering upgraded versions of our framework. First results of this work will be presented below in this paper.

The open architecture we have chosen implies to use externals tools, for analysis and evaluation on the one hand, for compiling and installing resources on the other hand. These tools may then be considered as black boxes, being externals commands called with convenient parameters. In particular, the Benchmarking Tool relies on two commands: the analyzer command, receiving input file as a parameter and producing the analyzed file, the evaluation command, receiving the analyzed file and the reference file as parameters and outputting counts of found, correct, found and correct items for each dimension. This allows, for example, to replace our

[2]http://www.qtsoftware.com/

analyzer with another one, by just wrapping the latter in a thin conversion layer to convert its inputs and its outputs.

2.2 Benchmarking Tool

The Benchmarking Tool, which architecture is depicted in Figure 1, is responsible of executing analysis and evaluation on pairs of data and reference files, using commands stored in benchmarking configuration. For each pair of files, the registered analysis command is executed followed by the evaluation one. In our case, those commands apply to the task of annotating files for syntactic chunks and dependencies.

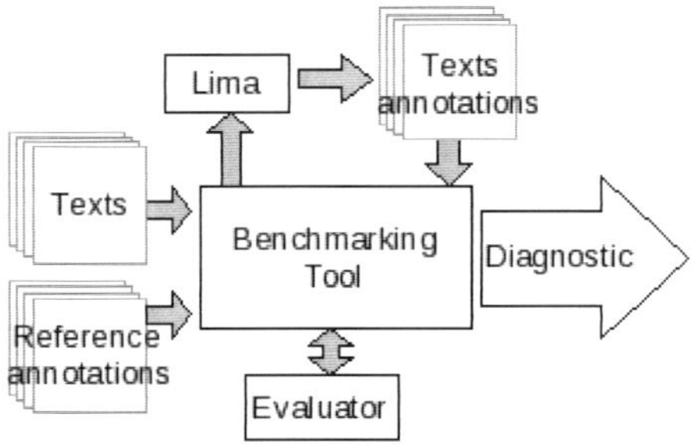

Figure 1: Benchmarking Tool data flow

We may consider the type of chunks and dependencies as dimensions of an evaluation. To a certain extent, these may be associated to linguistics phenomena which are tested, as proposed within the TSNLP project (Balkan et al., 1994) or, more recently, for Q/A systems by (Paiva et al., 2008). But in these projects, focus is also made on the evaluation tool, where we do not implement the evaluation tool but rely on an external program to provide accuracy of analysis.

The pairs of data and reference files are inserted inside a structure implemented as a pipeline, which may be modified (adding, removing, reordering units) with common GUI interfaces. After creation of the pipeline, the user may trigger a benchmarking (progress is shown by coloring pipeline units), which may be suspended, resumed or restarted at any moment. For note, the current version of the framework uses the local machine's processors to analyze pipeline units in parallel, but we intend to distribute the analyzes on the available nodes of a cluster soon. As soon as results are received, tables and graphics are updated on screen within a view showing previous and current results for each evaluated dimension. To refine diagnosis, the user may choose what dimensions are displayed, what metrics should be computed, and what pipeline units are used. Finally, any evaluation may be deleted if the corresponding modification did not increase performance and should be reverted.

Upon demand, the tool saves current benchmarking configuration and results as an XML file. Conversely, it loads a pipeline and results from file, so as to resume or switch between evaluations. The parsed output of the evaluator tool is recorded for each pipeline unit and for each dimension, so that metrics based on those quantities are computed for each pipeline unity or for the overall corpus. Besides, the date and a user comment for each evaluation are also saved for these records. Writing comments has proved to be very helpful to keep track of what changes have been made on code, linguistic resources, configuration, parameters, etc.

As an example within the Passage project, running evaluation with the Benchmarking Tool allowed us to notice that we had difficulties in recognizing verb-auxiliary dependencies. Considering previous results, we detected that this issue appeared after having introduced a set of idioms concerning pronominal verbs. Unit testing showed that the analysis of past perfect progressive for pronominal verbs was buggy. Patching the code gave us a 10 points f-measure gain for AUX-V dimension and 0.3 for all dependencies dimensions (AUX-V having a 2.6% global error rate within dependencies). Thus, benchmarking results have been saved with appropriate comment and other improvements or deficiencies could be examined.

With these features, the tool offers the possibility to have an overall view on evaluation results and on their evolution across time, given multiple data, dimensions of analysis and computed metrics. Therefore, it helps us, without any complex manipulation, to get a visual report on what implication on evaluation results has a modification to the analysis process. Furthermore, those tests allow to search for errors in resources as well as in code, so as to find how to enrich our linguistic resources or to identify deficiencies in our code.

Figure 2 shows a benchmarking using a set of 24 evaluation files (left part) to improve the analyzer's

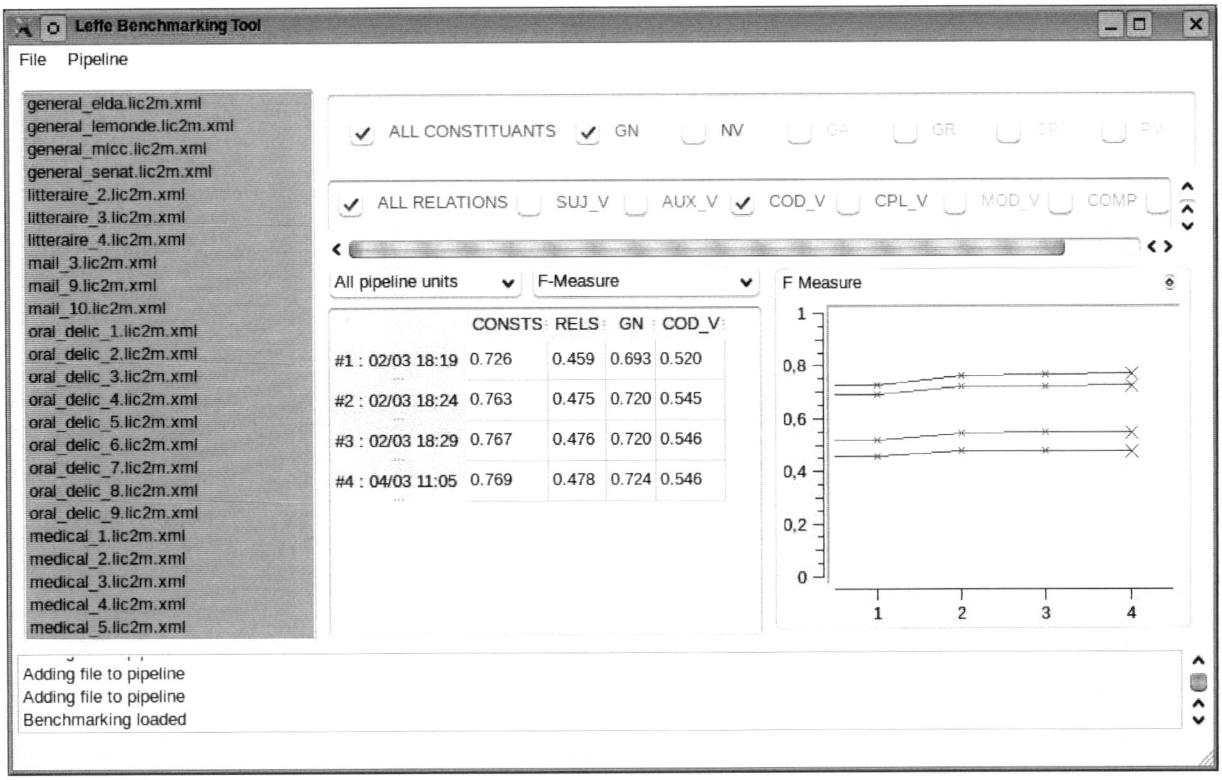

Figure 2: Chunks (CONSTS), dependencies (RELS), nominal chunks (GN) and direct objects dependencies (COD_V) f-measure results evolution through 4 evaluations on a 24 files corpus

results. The central table shows the measures corresponding to 4 successive evaluations, displaying results for the dimensions selected on the top most part (check-boxes). The right-hand side shows graphically the same data, successive evaluations being displayed as its abscissa and measures as its ordinate.

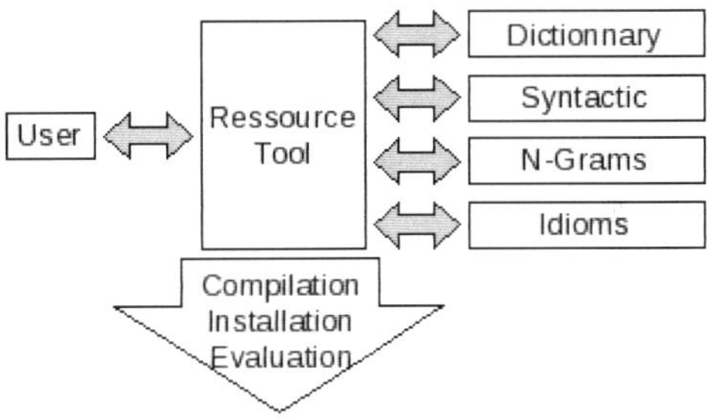

Figure 3: Resource Tool modular design

2.3 Resource Tool

The Resource Tool, which modular design is depicted in Figure 3, aims at making resources editing accessible for people who have neither a deep knowledge of the system internals nor computer programming skills. Enriching our resources implies having people, either specialized in linguistics or in testing to interact with the resources, even if not accustomed to our specific storage format for each resource.

In its current version, the Resource Tool allow to edit the following resources:

- Dictionary: items and their categories
- Syntactic rules: syntactic dependency detection
- Part-of-speech tagger learning corpus: tagged examples of *ngrams* disambiguation matrices
- Idioms: language dependent fixed expressions

Those resources are presented in a tabbed view, each having a dedicated interface and access functions. Within each resource, a search feature is implemented, which has shown to be really useful, especially for dictionary. The tool also provides simple means to save, compile and install resources, once they have been modified. This has to be very transparent for the user and we just provide a "Save" button and another "Compile and install" button. The current version of Resource Tool is quite ba-

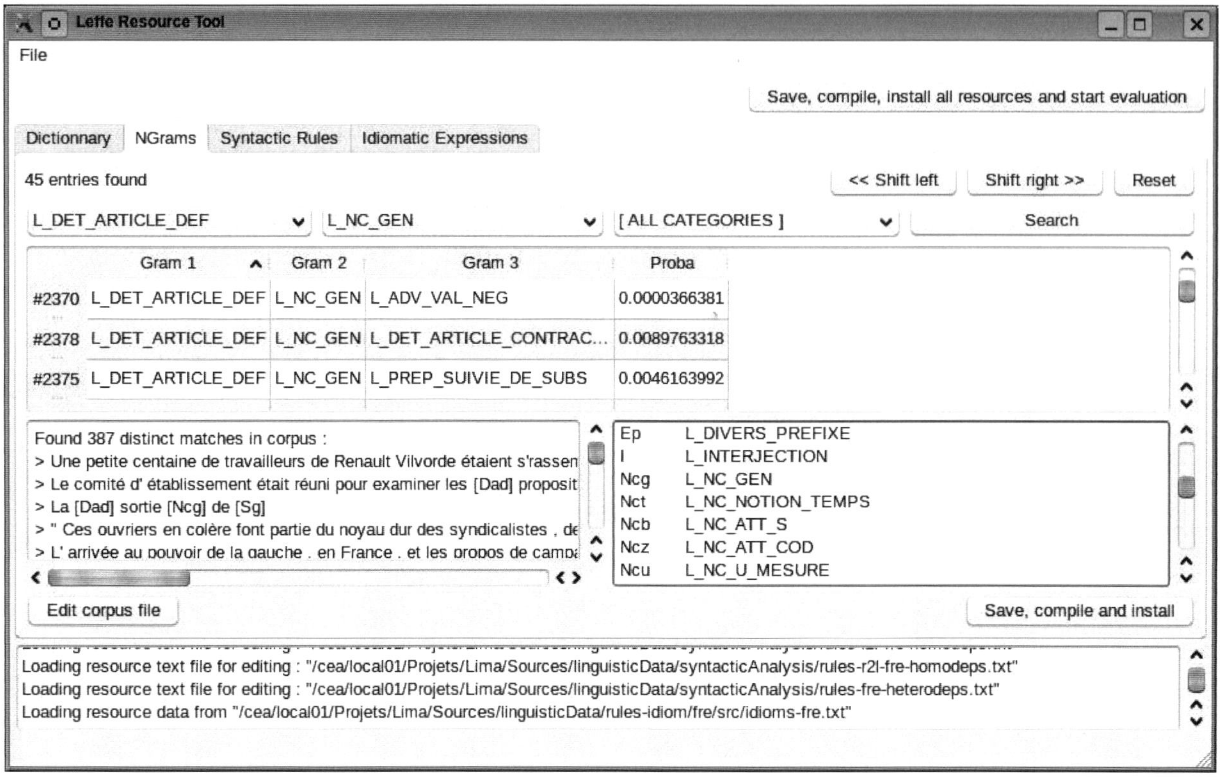

Figure 4: Viewing and editing disambiguation matrices: probabilities and examples for articles followed by nouns

sic in terms of edition capacities. Dictionary has a dedicated interface for editing words and their categories, but ngrams, syntactic rules and idioms resources may yet only be changed through a basic text editor.

Figure 4 shows the resource tool interface for the annotated corpus that allows to build part-of-speech disambiguation matrices. The top most tabs allow to switch between resources among editable ones. The data table shows the computed 3-grams (from our own tag set). The left part text field shows a list of sentences, where occurrences of the ngrams selected in the above table appear. The right part text field shows correspondences between two tag sets. Eventually, the "Edit corpus file" button opens an editor for the user to add sentences or to modify sentences in the tagged corpus.

The Resource Tool and the Benchmarking Tool communicate together through two signals: on the one hand when resources are installed, the Resource Tool may trigger an evaluation in the Benchmarking Tool, on the other hand when the evaluation has finished, the Resource Tool is notified and warns the user. Being aware of their respective status, we also warn the user for dangerous operations, like when trying to install resources while a benchmarking is still running, or when quitting the application before last benchmark is finished.

While these two applications are connected to be aware of benchmarking and resource installation status, no more interaction has been implemented for the moment to link evaluation and resource edition together. We have considered implementing a feature making possible to automatically do unit testing resource modifications, but, from our point of view, this has to be implemented with following restrictions: the Benchmarking Tool should remain generic (modifying configuration and resources should not be part of the tool) ; amount of required disk space should remain minimal (only differences between evaluations should be stored).

2.4 Preliminary results

We recently finished the first implementation iteration. The evaluator itself is provided by a partner laboratory. Its measurement methodology is deeply presented in (Paroubekr, 2006). From our point of view, we are only concerned in the fact that these

Chunks			Dependencies			Modifications
F	P	R	F	P	R	
72.6	72.0	73.2	45.9	54.2	39.8	Initial evaluation
76.3	76.2	76.3	47.5	56.1	41.1	Code reengineering / debugging
76.7	76.7	**76.7**	47.6	56.2	41.3	New set of syntactic rules
76.9	76.9	76.9	47.8	**56.7**	41.4	Specified preposition detection rules

Table 3: Benchmarking results, f-measure (F), precision (P), recall (R)

measures are relevant for improving the quality of analysis produced by our parser.

We applied our resource improvement methodology on a small annotated corpus of approximately 80.000 words, delivered after the EASy campaign, among 27 thematic files. For information, the whole process (analysis and evaluation for each file) is 5 minutes long on a bi-processor: this allows the software to be used intensively on a personal computer. Results in Table 3 show that the use of our framework already allowed us to introduce modifications of the linguistic resources with the Resource Tool; these changes lead to a slight improvement of the overall score of the system.

First, we obtained confirmation that some code reengineering and some debugging was required. These tasks, associated with iterative evaluation, have allowed us to detect parts of the code which did not give entire satisfaction, especially in the step transforming output from our analyzer to the expected Passage format. We also found a bug within the evaluation scripts, which, once corrected, forced to restart evaluation measures from the beginning: this shows the importance of having a stable environment apart analyzer (evaluation process, valid data and reference file). These results show that iterating over time and saving history may help to reveal potential weaknesses of the code and to detect what goes wrong.

Secondly, these tools where well-suited for evaluating the impact of a new set of syntactic rules, for which we did not have opportunities to do precise evaluation before. For this set of 20 rules, we systematically tried each rule separately, then kept the combination of the rules increasing scores. This improvement may appear as minimal, but these rules where written in the context of an ongoing work on our grammar. It gave an intuitive idea that this approach is not a dead-end and may be further explored. Besides, methodologies have been suggested to test the impact of each rule in the entire set of rules by systematically testing combinations of rules. But, currently, this is beyond our goal.

Finally, we also introduced some "syntactic sugar", by grouping some expressions within rules, and successfully obtained insurance that these modification did not lower scores. This is an important result for us in the sense that we ensure that the same set of rules expressed differently (with rules more concise thus more readable) do not introduce regressions.

3 Related works

We have previously described the test suite approach, along with the TSNLP project. This approach was concerned with identifying and systematically testing linguistic phenomena. As a conclusion of TSNLP, (Oepen et al., 1998) points out the necessity "to assess the impact of individual contributions, regularly evaluate the quality of the overall grammar, and compare it to previous versions". This project thus showed how positive it is to identify deficiencies and improve grammars by iterating tests over time. This is the goal we intend to reach with our framework.

More recently, in biomedical domain, (Baumgartner et al., 2008) describes implementation of a framework and, although it is applied to a text mining task, the approach remains quite close in its foundations (evaluation oriented, iterative testing, modular framework, open source, corpora based, etc.) to ours and encourages these kind of initiative by showing the importance of continuous evaluation while coding parser and engineering grammar. This work present the interest to rely on the UIMA framework, thus allowing a good modularity. In the future, we should study the interest to give the ability to our framework to integrate UIMA-ready modules.

Close to our Benchmarking Tool, some projects aim at building frameworks for text analysis, annotation and evaluation, which projects encourage people to use a common architecture, as openNLP or GATE. Those may also be used for benchmarking and evaluation tasks (Cunningham et al., 2002) as part of their process. But, while these framework often provide evaluation and regression testing tools, they are rarely well-suited for only implementing specific diagnostic tasks. We would appreciate that such frameworks focusing on evaluating, benchmarking and diagnosing, as generic as possible across IR tasks, become more widely available. If our Benchmarking Tool appears to be appropriate for other systems evaluations, we will consider making it available for the IR community.

4 Conclusions and future work

From our first use of the framework, we are convinced of the importance of diagnostic for accelerating the improvement of our analyzer, by making linguistic resources accessible and by iterating tests and comparing results obtained over time. We also concluded that this generic framework would be useful in other tasks, such as Information Retrieval. Especially, image retrieval is a very active and growing field of research, and we currently consider applying the Benchmarking Tool for accelerating the improvement of the image retrieval system developed in our laboratory (Joint et al., 2004).

This work also emphasizes the great distinction between performance evaluation and diagnostic evaluation. In our case, the association of the Benchmarking Tool and the Resource Tool used in conjunction with unit and regression testings helps to identify what part of the analysis process is concerned and, for grammar engineering, what rule or set of rules have to be questioned in order to improve the overall system performance.

Future directions of our work include the parallelization of the analysis on a cluster, so as to retrieve evaluation results as quickly as possible. This should allow us to use evaluation results from a larger annotated corpus. We also intend to focus on visualization of results for better identification and interpretation of errors, in order to access directly erroneous analysis and involved resources. A second development iteration will include the development of more user friendly resources editors.

We also plan to work on automatic syntactic rules inference, based on previous work in our laboratory (Embarek and Ferret, 2008). For this goal, continuous benchmarking will be even more important as the system will rely on experts tuning parameters for learning rules, the syntactic rules themselves being not necessarily edited nor viewable for the expert.

Acknowledgments

This work was partly funded by the French National Research Agency (ANR), MDCA program 2006.

References

Lorna Balkan, Klaus Netterz, Doug Arnold, Siety Meijer, 1994. *Test Suites for Natural Language Processing.* Proceedings of the Language Engineering Convention (LEC'94), 17–22.

William A Baumgartner, Kevin Bretonnel Cohen, Lawrence Hunter, 2008. *An open-source framework for large-scale, flexible evaluation of biomedical text mining systems.* Journal of Biomedical Discovery and Collaboration 2008, Vol. 3, pp 1.

Romaric Besançon, Gaël de Chalendar, 2005. *L'analyseur syntaxique de LIMA dans la campagne d'valuation EASY.* Actes des Ateliers de la 12e Confrence annuelle sur le Traitement Automatique des Langues Naturelles (TALN 2005), Vol. 2, pp 21.

John Carroll, Anette Frank, Dekang Lin, Detlef Prescher, Hans Uszkoreit, 2002. *Proceedings of the workshop beyond parseval - toward improved evaluation measures for parsing systems.* Proceedings of the 3rd International Conference on Language Resources and Evaluation (LREC'02).

Nikos Chatzichrisafis, Dick Crouch, Tracy Holloway King, Rowan Nairn, Manny Rayner, Marianne Santaholma, 2007. *Regression Testing For Grammar-Based Systems.* Proceedings of the GEAF07 Workshop, pp 128–143.

Eric V. de la Clergerie, Olivier Hamon, Djamel Mostefa, Christelle Ayache, Patrick Paroubek, Anne Vilnat, 2008. *PASSAGE: from French Parser Evaluation to Large Sized Treebank.* Proceedings of the Sixth International Language Resources and Evaluation (LREC'08).

Eric V. de la Clergerie, Christelle Ayache, Gaël de Chalendar, Gil Francopoulo, Claire Gardent, Patrick Paroubek, 2008. *Large scale production of syntactic annotations for French.* In Proceedings of the international workshop on Automated Syntactic Annotations for Interoperable Language Resources, Hong-Kong.

Hamish Cunningham, Diana Maynard, Kalina Bontcheva, Valentin Tablan, 2002. *GATE: A framework and graphical development environment for robust NLP tools and applications.* Proceedings of the 40th Anniversary Meeting of the ACL, 2002.

Mehdi Embarek, Olivier Ferret, 2008. *Learning patterns for building resources about semantic relations in the medical domain.* 6th Conference on Language Resources and Evaluation (LREC'08), Marrakech, Morocco.

Jonathan G. Fiscus, 1997. *A Post-Processing System to Yield Reduced Word Error Rates: Recognizer Output Voting Error Reduction (ROVER).* Proceedings IEEE Workshop on Automatic Speech Recognition and Understanding (ASRU97), pp 347–352.

Magali Joint, Pierre-Alain Moellic, Patrick Hede, Pascal Adam, 2004. *PIRIA: a general tool for indexing, search, and retrieval of multimedia content.* Proceedings of SPIE, Vol. 5298, 116 (2004), San Jose, CA, USA.

Sylvain Kahane, 2000. *Les grammaires de dpendance.* Traitement Automatique des Langues, Vol. 41.

Stephan Oepen, Daniel P. Flickinger, 1998. *Towards systematic grammar profiling. Test suite technology ten years after.* Special Issue on Evaluation 12, 411–436.

Valeria de Paiva, Tracy Holloway King, 2008. *Designing Testsuites for Grammar-based Systems in Applications.* Proceedings of the GEAF08 Workshop, pp 49–56.

Patrick Paroubek, Isabelle Robba, Anne Vilnat, Christelle Ayache, 2006. *Data, Annotations and Measures in EASY, the Evaluation Campaign for Parsers of French.* 5th Conference on Language Resources and Evaluation (LREC'06), Genoa, Italy.

C. J. van Rijsbergen, 1979. *Information Retrieval, 2nd edition.*

Integrating High Precision Rules with Statistical Sequence Classifiers for Accuracy and Speed

Wenhui Liao, Marc Light, and Sriharsha Veeramachaneni
Research and Development,Thomson Reuters
610 Opperman Drive, Eagan MN 55123

Abstract

Integrating rules and statistical systems is a challenge often faced by natural language processing system builders. A common subclass is integrating high precision rules with a Markov statistical sequence classifier. In this paper we suggest that using such rules to constrain the sequence classifier decoder results in superior accuracy and efficiency. In a case study of a named entity tagging system, we provide evidence that this method of combination does prove efficient than other methods. The accuracy was the same.

1 Introduction

Sequence classification lies at the core of several natural language processing applications, such as named entity extraction, Asian language segmentation, Germanic language noun decompounding, and event identification. Statistical models with a Markov dependency have been successful employed to perform these tasks, e.g., hidden Markov models (HMMs)(Rabiner, 1989) and conditional random fields (CRFs)(Lafferty et al., 2001). These statistical systems employ a Viterbi (Forney, 1973) decoder at runtime to efficiently calculate the most likely label sequence based on the observed sequence and model. Statistical machine translation systems make use of similar decoders.

In many situations it is beneficial, and sometimes required, for these systems to respect constraints from high precision rules. And thus when building working sequence labeling systems, researchers/software engineers are often faced with the task of combining these two approaches. In this paper we argue for a particular method of combining statistical models with Markov dependencies and high precision rules. We outline a number of ways to do this and then argue that guiding the decoder of the statistical system has many advantages over other methods of combination.

But first, does the problem of combining multiple approaches really happen? In our experience the need arises in the following way: a statistical approach with a Markov component is chosen because it has the best precision/recall characteristics and has reasonable speed. However, a number of rules arise for varied reasons. For example, the customer provides domain knowledge not present in the training data or a particular output characteristic is more important that accuracy. Consider the following fictitious but plausible situation: A named entity tagging system is built using a CRF. The customer then provides a number of company names that cannot be missed, i.e., false negatives for these companies are catastrophic but false positives can be tolerated. In addition, it is known that, unlike in the training data, the runtime data will have a company name immediately before every ticker symbol. The question facing the builder of the system is how to combine the CRF with rules based on the must-find company list and the company-name-before-every-ticker-symbol fact.

Similar situations arise for the other sequence tagging situations mentioned above and for machine translation. We suspect that even for non-language applications, such as gene sequence labeling, similar situations arise.

Proceedings of the NAACL HLT Workshop on Software Engineering, Testing, and Quality Assurance for Natural Language Processing, pages 74–77,
Boulder, Colorado, June 2009.

In the next section we will discuss a number of methods for combining statistical systems and high precision rules and argue for guiding the decoder of the statistical model. Then in section 3, we describe an implementation of the approach and give evidence that the speed benefits are substantial.

2 Methods for Combining a Markov Statistical System and High Precision Rules

One method of combination is to encode high precision rules as features and then train a new model that includes these features. One advantage is that the system stays a straightforward statistical system. In addition, the rules are fully integrated into the system allowing the statistical model weigh the rules against other evidence. However, the model may not give the rules high weight if training data does not bear out their high precision or if the rule trigger does not occur often enough in the training data. Thus, despite a "rule" feature being on, the system may not "follow" the rule in its result labeling. Also, addition or modification of a rule would require a retraining of the model for optimal accuracy. The retraining process may be costly and/or may not be possible in the operational environment.

Another method is to run both the statistical system and the rules and then merge the resulting labels giving preference to the labels resulting from the high precision rules. The benefits are that the rules are always followed. However, the statistical system does not have the information needed to give an optimal solution based on the results of the high precision rules. In other words, the results will be inconsistent from the view of the statistical system; *i.e.*, if it had know what the rules were going to say, then it would have calculated the remaining part of the label sequence differently. In addition, the decoder considers part of the label sequence search space that is only going to be ruled out, pun intended, later.

Now for the preferred method: run the rules first, then use their output to guide the decoder for the statistical model. The benefits of this method are that the rules are followed, the statistical system is informed of constraints imposed by the rules and thus the statistical system calculates optimal paths given these constraints. In addition, the decoder considers only those label sequences consistent with these constraints, resulting in a smaller search space. Thus, we would expect this method to produce both a more accurate and a faster implementation.

Consider Figure 1 which shows a lattice that represents all the labeling sequences for the input ... *Microsoft on Monday announced a* ... The possible labels are O (out), P (person), C (company), L (location) . Assume *Microsoft* is in a list of must-find companies and that *on* and *Monday* are part of a rule that makes them NOT names in this context. The bold points are constraints from the high-precision rules. In other words, only sequences that include these bold points need to be considered.

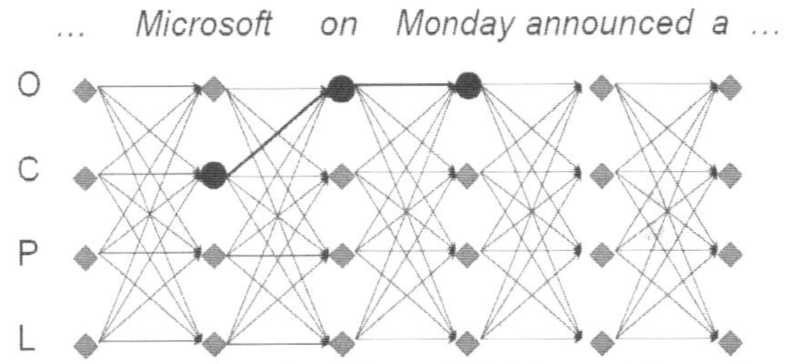

Figure 1: Guiding decoding with high-precision rules

Figure 1 also illustrates how the constraints reduce the search space. Without constraints, the search space includes $4^6 = 4096$ sequences, while with constraints, it includes only $4^3 = 64$.

It should also be noted that we do not claim to have invented the idea of constraining the decoder. For example, in the context of active learning, where a human corrects some of the errors made by a CRF sequence classifier, (Culota et al., 2006) proposed a constrained Viterbi algorithm that finds the path with maximum probability that passes through the labels assigned by the human. They showed that constraining the path to respect the human labeling considerably improves the accuracy on the remaining tokens in the sequence. Our contribution is noticing that constraining the decoder is a good way to integrate rule output.

3 A Case Study: Named Entity Recognition

In this section, we flesh out the discussion of named entity (NE) tagging started above. Since the entity type of a word is determined mostly by the context of the word, NE tagging is often posed as a sequence classification problem and solved by Markov statistical systems.

3.1 A Named Entity Recognition System

The system described here starts with a CRF which was chosen because it allows for the use of numerous and arbitrary features of the input sequence and it can be efficiently trained and decoded. We used the Mallet toolkit (McCallum, 2002) for training the CRF but implemented our own feature extraction and runtime system. We used standard features such as the current word, the word to the right/left, orthographic shape of the word, membership in word sets (e.g., common last names), features of neighboring words, etc.

The system was designed to run on news wire text and based on this data's characteristics, we designed a handful of high precision rules including:

***Rule 1**: if a token is in a must-tag list, this token should be marked as Company no matter what the context is.*

***Rule 2**: if a capitalized word is followed by certain company suffix such as **Ltd, Inc, Corp**, etc., label both as Company.*

***Rule 3**: if a token sequence is in a company list and the length of the sequence is larger than 3, label them as Company.*

***Rule 4**: if a token does not include any uppercase letters, is not pure number, and is not in an exceptions list, label it as not part of a name. (The exceptions list includes around 70 words that are not capitalized but still could be an NE, such as **al, at, in, -**, etc.)*

***Rule 5**: if a token does not satisfy rule 4 but its neighboring tokens satisfy rule 4, then if this token is a time related word, label it as not part of a name. (Example time tokens are **January** and **Monday**.)*

The first three rules aim to find company names and the last two to find tokens that are *not* part of a name.

These rules are integrated into the system as described in section 2: we apply the rules to the input token sequence and then use the resulting labels, if any, to constrain the Viterbi decoder for the CRF.

A further optimization of the system is based on the following observation: features need not be calculated for tokens that have already received labels from the rules. (An exception to this is when features are copied to a neighbor, e.g., the token to my left is a number.) Thus, we do not calculate many features of rule-labeled tokens. Note that feature extraction can often be a major portion of the computational cost of sequence labeling systems (see Table 1(b))

3.2 Evidence of Computational Savings Resulting from Our Proposed Method of Integration

We compare the results when high-precision rules are integrated into CRF for name entity extraction (company, person, and location) in terms of both accuracy and speed for different corpora. Three corpora are used, CoNLL (CoNLL 2003 English shared task official test set), MUC (Message Understanding Conference), and TF (includes around 1000 news articles from Thomson Financial).

Table 1(a) shows the results for each corpora respectively. The baseline method does not use any high-precision rules, the Post-corr uses the high-precision rules to correct the labeling from the CRF, and Constr-viti uses the rules to constrain the label sequences considered by the Viterbi decoder. In general, Constr-viti achieves slightly better precision and recall.

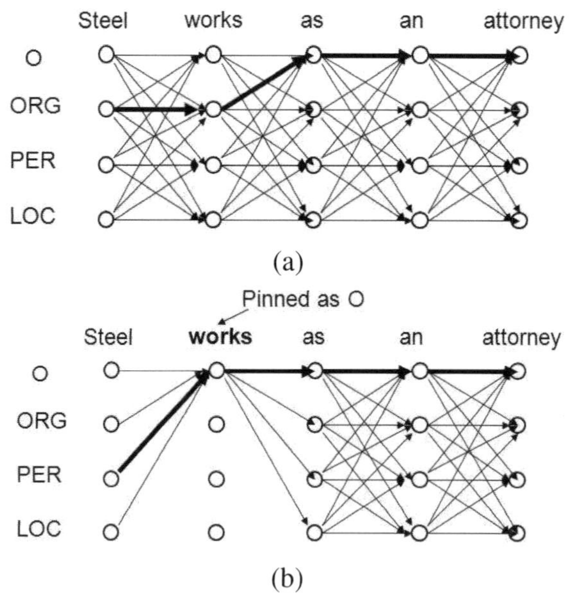

Figure 2: (b) A test example : (a) without constraints; (b) with constraints

To better understand how our strategy could improve the accuracy, we did some analysis on the

Table 1: Experiment Results

Database	Methods	Precision	Recall	F1
CoNLL	Baseline	84.38	83.02	83.69
	Post-corr	85.87	84.86	85.36
	Constr-viti	**85.98**	**85.55**	**85.76**
TF	Baseline	**88.39**	82.42	85.30
	Post-corr	87.69	88.30	87.99
	Constr-viti	88.02	**88.54**	**88.28**
MUC	Baseline	**92.22**	88.72	**90.43**
	Post-Corr	91.28	88.87	90.06
	Constr-viti	90.86	**89.37**	90.11

(a)Precision and Recall

Methods	Rules	Features	Viterbi	Overall
Baseline	0	0.78	0.22	1
Post-corr	0.08	0.78	0.22	1.08
Constr-vite	0.08	0.35	0.13	**0.56**
Baseline	0	0.85	0.15	1
Post-Corr	0.14	0.85	0.15	1.14
Constr-vite	0.14	0.38	0.1	**0.62**
Baseline	0	0.79	0.21	1
Post-corr	0.12	0.79	0.21	1.12
Constr-vite	0.12	0.36	0.12	**0.60**

(b)Time Efficiency

testing data. In one example as shown in Figure 2, *Steel works as an attorney*, without high-precision rules, *Steel works* is tagged as a company since it is in our company list. Post-correction changes the label of *works* to O, but it is unable to fix *Steel*. With our strategy, since *works* is pinned as O in the Vertibi algorithm, *Steel* is tagged as Per. Thus, compared to post-correction, the advantage of constraining Viterbi is that it is able to affect the whole path where the token is, instead a token itself. However, the improvements were not significant in our case study. We have not done an error analysis. We can only speculate that the high precision rules do not have perfect precision and thus create a number of errors that the statistical model would not have made on its own.

We also measured how much the constrained Viterbi method improves efficiency. We divide the computational time to three parts: time in applying rules, time in feature extraction, and time in Viterbi computation. Table 1(b) lists the time efficiency. Instead using specific time unit (e.g. second), we use ratio instead by assuming the overall time for the baseline method is 1. As shown in the table, for the three data sets, the overall time of our method is 0.56, 0.62, and 0.60 of the time of the baseline algorithm respectively. The post-correction method is the most expensive one because of the extra time spending in rules. Overall, the constrained Viterbi method is substantially faster than the Baseline and Post-corr methods in addition to being more accurate.

4 Conclusions

The contribution of this paper is the repurposing of the idea of constraining a decoder: we constrain the decoder as a way to integrate high precision rules with a statistical sequence classifier. In a case study of named entity tagging, we show that this method of combination does in fact increase efficiency more than competing methods without any lose of accuracy. We believe analogous situations exist for other sequence classifying tasks such as Asian language segmentation, Germanic language noun decompounding, and event identification.

References

Aron Culota, Trausti Kristjansson, Andrew McCallum, and Paul Viola. 2006. Corrective feedback and persistent learning for information extraction. *Artificial Intelligence Journal*, 170:1101–1122.

G. D. Forney. 1973. The viterbi algorithm. *Proceedings of the IEEE*, 61(3):268–278.

John Lafferty, Andrew McCallum, and Fernando Pereira. 2001. Conditional random fields: Probabilistic models for segmenting and labeling sequence data. In *Proc. 18th International Conf. on Machine Learning*, pages 282–289.

A.K. McCallum. 2002. Mallet: A machine learning for language toolkit. http://mallet.cs.umass.edu.

Lawrence R. Rabiner. 1989. A tutorial on hidden markov models and selected applications in speech recognition. *Proceedings of the IEEE*, pages 257–286.

Author Index